EARLY CHILDHOOD EDU
Leslie R. Williams, Editor Milli
ADVISORY BOARD: Barbara T. Bowman, Harr
Doris Pronin Fromberg, Celia Genishi, Sta
Alice Sterling Honig, Elizabeth Jones, G.

(Continued)

Diversity in the Classroom

New Approaches to the Education of Young Children

Second Edition

FRANCES E. KENDALL

Foreword by
CAROL BRUNSON PHILLIPS

Teachers College, Columbia University
New York and London

Published by Teachers College Press, 1234 Amsterdam Avenue, New York, NY 10027

Excerpt from "Reassurance" in *Revolutionary Petunias & Other Poems,* copyright (c) 1972 by Alice Walker, reprinted by permission of Harcourt Brace & Company. Reprinted in the U.K. and the British Commonwealth by permission of The Women's Press.

Photo credits: The photo on p. 113 was taken by Deborah Ehrens; all others were taken by Anita Schriver.

Library of Congress Cataloging-in-Publication Data
Kendall, Frances E.
    Diversity in the classroom: new approaches to the education of
young children/Frances E. Kendall. — 2nd ed.
    p.   cm. — (Early childhood education series)
Includes bibliographical references and index.
    ISBN 0-8077-3498-5 (paper: alk. paper)
    1. Multicultural education—United States. 2. Early childhood
education—United States. I. Title II. Series
    LC1099.3K45 1996
    370.19'6—dc20   95-44248

Printed on acid-free paper
Manufactured in the United States of America
03 02 01 00 99 98 97 96   8 7 6 5 4 3 2 1

This book is dedicated to Marie Jones who came into my life when I was seven and, by her nature and example, made me question the messages I was receiving about race. She continues to be a powerful force of love in my life.

Contents

Foreword

Twelve years ago, when the first edition of this book appeared, Dr. Frances Kendall hoped it could help change the way we approached multicultural education in the early school years, such that the consequence of our work would be social justice. Funny. Who would have predicted then that, nearly 15 years later she would need to fashion an even bolder challenge to us to make this consequence possible?

But she does. For we are reminded that, even though in the last decade we have removed those overt, outward obstacles to social justice that could be legislated and regulated away, there remain more subtle and covert ones, whose increasingly dire consequences can be seen in the lives of culturally and racially diverse children. There is more infant mortality, more teen pregnancy, more school failure, more youth alcohol and drug abuse, more abuse and neglect. Pick any indicator for the quality of life for children and you will find children of color at the highest levels of distress.

So Dr. Kendall's approach asks us to engage more deeply in the activities that will be required to address squarely the "isms" in their most complicated and confounding form—activities like emotional risktaking. In a comfortably simple, yet unusually profound way, she asks us to join her on a journey toward eliminating those things that allow the institutional forms of bias and exclusion to play themselves out, unabated, such as the self-fulfilling prophesy that can rise from our attitudes and expectations.

I remember a front page article in a Los Angeles newspaper about an 8th-grade graduation party. It was given by some Hollywood movie stars for a class of low-income Black youngsters in Watts. The newspaper praised the motivation of the party sponsors to acknowledge this event in the lives of these children. Why? Because this "was probably the last graduation these kids would ever have." I remember thinking how subtly the message was conveyed to the readers of the low expectation for these kids' futures.

In my 25 years in early childhood education, I have watched this lack of faith in children played out in the educational literature. I have watched as African American youngsters were called "culturally deprived," then called "educationally disadvantaged," and now the current more polite but even more devastating label—"at risk." Being labeled "at risk" is like being voted least likely to succeed. *And, where there is no faith in your future success, there is no real effort to pave the way for it.*

I can't imagine losing this generation of children to welfare dependency, to homelessness, to chronic and disabling illness, to prison, or to death before they reach adulthood. My heart tells me that it is not possible and that we will take up the challenge that Dr. Kendall so succinctly and tenaciously puts before us—to deconstruct old ideas as well as construct new ones.

Can we really achieve social justice for children? Yes. If, as we are asked, we make it possible through our collective will.

— Carol Brunson Phillips
Executive Director
Council for Early Childhood Professional Recognition

Acknowledgments

Late one night as I was eating take-out Chinese food in my office and correcting the draft of this edition of *Diversity in the Classroom* for the final, final time, my fortune cookie presented me with this: "You should be able to undertake and complete anything." And a voice in my head said, "Not without a whole lot of help!"

I am extremely blessed with a community of colleagues, friends, and "family" who have offered me the benefit of their tough minds and good hearts. While I thank the following by name, many others contributed to my well-being and clear thinking. I am deeply appreciative.

Two serendipitous yet pivotal conversations moved my thinking to a whole new place: Janet Bagby, with whom I have shared only telephone conversations and faxes, encouraged me to deconstruct my assumptions about child development; Cecelia Alvarado Kuster pushed me to rethink what it *really* means to be mindful of children's culture as we teach them.

Several people dropped everything to give advice, point me in a new direction, send research, or listen to a paragraph: Carol Brunson Phillips, David Tulin, Phaizon Wood, and Ann Sims were never too busy to help.

Ann Benjamin's ability to pick up a 13-year-old conversation without skipping a beat reflects the strong base of respect and friendship created in my years at Tufts. Though she was "the student" and I was "the professor," we learned from each other as happens in the best of instances.

Tiny Tots Play Center, Bayshore Child Care Center, and Camp Perple generously allowed pictures to be taken and used in this new edition.

Diane Davenport, my friend and favorite librarian, cheerfully provided me with a million-and-a-half answers—references, dates, articles, and random information.

To say to someone, "I never could have done it without you," sounds glib. In Susan Rawlin's case, it is true. For years she has looked at everything I have written with her keen understanding of language and a sharp pencil.

Jayne Schabel typed, researched, and took care of the details of my work life so that I could write without interruptions.

Working with Teachers College Press has been a true collaboration. Susan Liddicoat has been tireless in looking for information I couldn't find, adroitly correcting drafts, and nudging me gently along. Leslie Williams encouraged me to say what I believe to be true rather than sugarcoat my words to make the readers less uncomfortable. I am proud to be one of their authors.

Finally, three were steadfast, loving, and my foundation of support: Hilde, my Irish terrier pal; Julie Silber, who is not only a wonderful listener but also tells great jokes; and Anita Schriver, a brilliant teacher and fine human being, whose commitment to children and social justice is unwavering. She is my hero.

Diversity in the Classroom

New Approaches to the Education of Young Children

Second Edition

Journeys Toward an Unknown Future

The metaphor of journeys keeps arising as I think about the 12 years since the first edition of *Diversity in the Classroom* was published. And, while many of the journeys on which we embark have known destinations, the national, professional, and personal paths on which we now find ourselves are filled with struggle without our knowing exactly what we are moving toward. In some ways we are taking a leap of faith. Nationally, we are clearly in the throes of figuring out how we will respond to the needs of a population far more diverse than that of any other time in our history. As a nation (and I believe as a planet), we must figure out how to live interdependently, understanding that, if we can't, we may not survive.

Extremely serious questions face us daily: How can we create a *United* States from a massive collection of peoples who want to retain their own cultural values and beliefs? Should we have an "official" language, English, forcing those for whom English is not their first language to assimilate and acculturate immediately and to give up their own languages? Do immigrants, both legal and undocumented, have rights to health care, public education, and social services formerly accorded to all? How will we assure that gay men and lesbians are treated fairly in a country that is at odds about their very existence?

We must carefully study the civil-rights issues connected to each question. Should we withhold access to education, health care, housing and employment, and freedom from discrimination from any group of people because we are uncomfortable with who they are or where they come from? How will we deal with the escalating disparities of life expectancy, level of income, and access to life-sustaining employment between poor and wealthy, and Whites and people of color (particularly African Americans and Latinos)? How will we educate a population whose skills we need now more than ever as we rapidly move into a highly technical world? Will higher education become the domain of only the rich? How will we respond as a nation to rising violence? Obviously, these questions are not all new, and there are no easy answers. What we do know is that we no longer have the luxury of ignoring the questions.

Those of us in early childhood education are experiencing this national journey in both philosophical and concrete ways. The field as a whole is facing theoretical dilemmas as it reexamines the role of culture in the development of children and struggles to define what *developmentally appropriate* means and for whom. Teachers and other caregivers are working to integrate an anti-bias, multicultural approach into the overall curriculum and everyday interactions with children and parents. We are also struggling to create a curriculum that prepares children for a multicultural world. In some schools, many languages and cultures are represented, and that makes the changes in our school population all the more apparent and the needs more immediate.

MY JOURNEY

My own journey is the direct result of my being a White, Southern, upper-middle-class woman. I was raised in Waco, Texas. The messages I received from my family and those around us were that Black people were not like us, less than human, not as good as we were. But the Black woman my mother hired as a maid became the significant adult in my life. My confusion became profound; I suffered from what we now call "cognitive dissonance." On one hand, my culture gave me very clear signals that Black people were not to be trusted; on the other, there were many times when I felt a Black woman was the only person I could count on.

In 1961 I left Waco and went to Washington, D.C. Since my father had taught in a boy's prep school, it had always been assumed that I would go away for my secondary education. I attended National Cathedral, an Episcopal girls' school that sits in the shadow of the Washington Cathedral, to which it is connected. This was, of course, at the height of the Civil Rights movement, and the Cathedral was a center of civil-rights activity. On a weekly basis I heard from the Episcopal church that social-justice activities were an essential part of being Christian. And further, for the first time in my life, I was in school with Black girls who were from the same socioeconomic class as I and who were a lot smarter.

During my high school years I spent less and less time at home, thinking that if I absented myself geographically I could leave my history behind.

I was horrified when my mother told me that my great-grandparents had owned slaves; my family was, and still is, in the cotton business—a business that was built on the backs of people who benefited little from their labor. I carried the burden of guilt for my family's behavior. I felt I had to right all of their wrongs. Beginning in college, the National Student YWCA gave me a place to explore my own racism and to begin to understand how institutional racism functions. I grew to believe that, with a great deal of intentional work, it is possible to change both oneself and institutions. (I am grateful that I no longer feel I must make reparation for my ancestors' behavior. I do still believe, however, that I am responsible for making change using the economic and social privileges I inherited.)

At Bank Street College, a graduate school of education in New York City, my arena for antiracism work became early childhood education, and I began to create antiracist, anti-bias curricula. After teaching 3-, 4-, and 5-year-olds at a demonstration day-care center in Brooklyn, I returned to the South, to the University of North Carolina at Chapel Hill, to get a Ph.D. and to figure out what it means for me to be White and Southern. The easy part was the Ph.D. The difficult work was looking at elements of myself and my history that were unspeakably painful. How was it possible that people who were just like me were members of the Ku Klux Klan? How could they have treated Black people so inhumanely for so many decades? How would I live a different life? In *Talking Back,* bell hooks (1989) quotes Buddhist Thich Nhat Hanhn on "restoring the self to a condition of wholeness":

In French they have a word *recueillement* to describe the attitude of someone
trying to be himself or herself, not to be dispersed, one member of the body
here, another there. One tries to recover, to be once more in good shape,
to become whole again. (p. 29)

I grew to love North Carolina and the people there, and I made peace with
the fact that I will work on my own racism until long after I'm dead.

     After teaching for 3 years at Tufts University in the Eliot Pearson Depart-
ment of Child Study, I moved to California's Bay Area. Understanding that my
passion lay in working with others on the complicated issue of racism, I began
a consulting firm in 1982. Since then I have broadened my work to address
organizational change as I help academic and corporate clients create structures
and environments that are hospitable to all who work in them. My journey, like
the nation's and early childhood education's, continues. I learn much more
from working with my clients than they could possibly learn from me.

THE CRITICAL ROLE OF THE TEACHER

On February 29, 1968, the National Advisory Commission on Civil Disor-
ders (the Kerner Commission) warned that the United States was "moving
toward two societies, one black, one white—separate and unequal." Twenty
years later, the Kerner Commission repeated its concerns that, while some
gains had been made, the educational and economic gaps between Black
and White people were, in fact, wider than they had been in 1968 (Bernstein, 1988). In short, racism is *still* one of the most crippling diseases from
which this country suffers. It affects each of us, regardless of color, race,
class, gender, age, or sexual orientation.

     The second edition of this book underscores my belief that education
can be a powerful force in the struggle to eliminate all forms of institutional discrimination. Both adults and children are involved in reaching this goal.
As members of the educational system, teachers can work toward the elimination of racism by examining their own roles in the perpetuation of institutional racism. I hold the following values regarding the role of the teacher:

- Teachers are models for children; as models, they should show respect
  and concern for all people.
- Teachers provide experiences through which children can begin to
  develop their own values.
- Teachers encourage children to explore, to initiate, to question, to
  grapple with tough questions, and to be active rather than passive
  learners.
- Teachers are active participants in children's learning.

- Teachers pass their own values and attitudes on to children both intentionally and unintentionally; therefore it is important that they be keenly aware of their own attitudes and values.

Thus I had two purposes in writing this book: first, to help teachers identify their own attitudes and biases and examine ways in which these attitudes affect their teaching, and, second, to help teachers use a multicultural approach to education regardless of the racial or ethnic compositions of their classes. Children have the right to experience the affirmation of individual differences and respect for the cultural heritages of all people.

The foundation for the first edition of *Diversity in the Classroom* lay solely in the developmental–interaction philosophy of education as defined by Shapiro and Biber (1972) and in Hilda Taba's (1955) philosophy of education for human relations. This edition builds on those theoretical frameworks and incorporates the more culturally contextual perspectives of Michael Cole, Howard Gardner, and Lev Vygotsky, among others. The developmental–interaction philosophy addresses the thinking (cognitive) and feeling (affective) aspects of the child's growth, the influences of culture and experience on a child's development, and how they shape the education experience. Shapiro and Biber are very clear that "the implementation of the goals [of the developmental–interaction philosophy] must be differentiated according to the social, cultural, and developmental status of the child population involved" (p. 61). Taba speaks to the importance of working against ethnocentricity in children and the necessity of helping young children learn to explore feelings and information, to consider alternative approaches and possibilities when solving problems and disputes, and to analyze their own and others' beliefs and values.

The manifestations of institutional racism within schools today are more subtle than the blatant legal segregation abolished by the 1954 Supreme Court decision *Brown v. Board of Education*. As it has become legally unacceptable to support overt racism, the attitudes that were responsible for creating segregation have been driven underground. Despite superficial changes in behavior, many underlying attitudes remain the same. A situation now exists that encourages change in teachers' actions without providing support for changes in beliefs. The result may be that teachers are sending children double messages. That is, even though a teacher may be conscientious in providing materials and information about a variety of cultural, ethnic, and racial groups, her or his own acts may reveal very different feelings than those that she or he professes. The following story illustrates what I am talking about.

A White teacher worked in a very prestigious child care center in a progressive university community. The center was well known for its strong multicultural emphasis; the teacher had spent a great deal of money on books, equipment and materials. Because the program was thought of so highly, the teacher was asked if it would be possible to make a videotape of her center to use in teacher-training classes. The teacher was pleased to have her program used as a model and the filming took place. When the teacher and the filmmakers looked at the video, they saw many good books, games, and pictures. They also noticed something the teacher had not been aware of: after every time she touched a Black child, she washed her hands.

The children in the center were aware on some level of what she was doing. Young children pick up messages from *all* of adults' behaviors, not just the ones of which we want them to be conscious. While the teacher was telling the children that variety in people is good, that we should value and respect others for their similarities and differences, she was showing them the opposite.

There are many other ways in which we send double messages, though they may be less dramatic than that of the teacher in the story. Whom we call on (and whom we don't), how we compose activity groups, whom we praise and for what, all may underscore the belief, conscious or unconscious, that some children are incapable of high academic performance due to their race or culture. Research on the effects of teachers' expectations on student behavior and ability has spanned almost 30 years. Robert Rosenthal identified what he called the "Pygmalion effect," that people achieve at the level to which they are expected to achieve (Rosenthal & Jacobsen, 1968). Some of the studies done on teachers' expectations have found that they have lower expectations of children of color and poor White children than they have for White middle-class children (Minuchin & Shapiro, 1983). In 1987, another study was done which showed that teacher expectations become a self-fulfilling prophecy even when the expectations are groundless (Rosenthal, 1987). Thus negative attitudes may show themselves in ways more subtle than segregation but no less destructive. As noted previously, a goal of *Diversity in the Classroom* is to encourage teachers constantly to monitor their thoughts and behaviors for race-, gender-, class-, and physical ability-based expectations, whether positive or negative. This ongoing assessment of our attitudes and behaviors is part of the journey on which teachers must embark. Unless they understand the complexities and the deadly, pervasive nature of institutional racism, sexism, heterosexism, and so on, teachers will be unable to create truly multicultural educational environments for their students.

MULTICULTURAL EDUCATION

Prior to the 1960s, education in the United States focused on the growth and development of White children. In his booklet *The 'Rightness' of 'Whiteness': The World of the White Child in a Segregated Society,* Abraham Citron (1971) describes

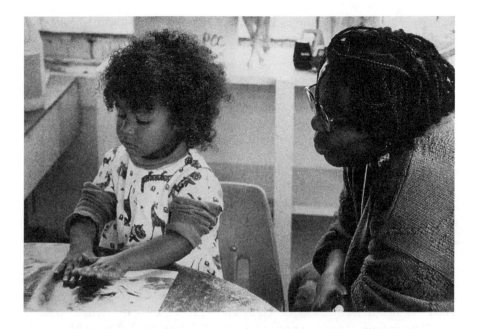

the skewed experiences of White and Black children in a world in which the only people pictured are White. One need only visualize the first-grade readers of the 1950s and 1960s with Dick and Jane, Mom and Dad, Spot and Puff—all white (except Spot), all living in a white house with a white picket fence—to understand the messages given to White children (you are regular, normal children) and to Black children (you do not exist). In response to issues raised by the Civil Rights movement and the Kerner Commission Report, in the mid-to-late 1960s the focus of education broadened to include the "compensatory" schooling of Black children who were labeled "disadvantaged" and "culturally deprived." While the emphasis on "multicultural education" was still 5 years away, this shift in focus marked a beginning. Theorists in the 1970s (Banks, 1973; Gay, 1973; Gold, Grant, & Rivlin, 1977; Youngblood, 1979) prescribed a new approach to education, one in which cultural diversity is affirmed and actively supported in the classroom.

In order to clarify the different educational philosophies and practices that were being called "multicultural education," Christine Sleeter and Carl Grant (1994) devised a "typology of approaches" to "multicultural education." I include it here for two reasons: first, because I think it is helpful to understand the range of methods you might use in addressing issues of difference in your classroom. Second, it is important for me to be clear about my own position in this typology so that you are able to take my biases into account as you read. Sleeter and Grant have identified five approaches to multicultural education, each with its own goals and practices. The first three

were most prominent in the 1960s, but many teachers continue to view multicultural education in these ways.

1. Teaching the Exceptional and Culturally Different
2. Human Relations
3. Single-Group Studies
4. Multicultural Education
5. Education That Is Multicultural and Social Reconstructionist

The goal of the Teaching the Exceptional and Culturally Different
approach is to help those who are different from mainstream America due
to race, culture, and/or language "become equipped with the cognitive
skills, concepts, information, language, and values required by American
society in order to hold a job and function within the society's existing institutions and culture" (Sleeter & Grant, 1994, p. 42). Teachers who practice
this approach fall into two groups: those who view differences as negatives
to be eliminated, and others who see differences merely as differences. The
first group develops a curriculum that compensates for the children's perceived deficiencies and lack of "traditional American" experiences and values. The second group acknowledges the differences that exist and works
to provide children with a new set of skills so that they can be assimilated
into American society. The common feature between the groups is the goal
of assimilation. This approach to multicultural education, however, should
not be confused with the belief that poor White children and those of color
must be taught how to survive in a middle-class White society; in this latter
approach, the children are not seen as "exceptional" but rather as under the
control of a system that is hostile to them. For further discussion of this
issue, see the consideration of Delpit's (1988) work in the section on Language Arts in Chapter 7.

Teachers who choose the Human Relations approach generally focus
on tolerance and appreciation of others. Their goal is to create a classroom
everyone feels good about being in. The curriculum includes working on
stereotypes and promoting unity among the children. "Human Relations
deals with self-concept [and self-esteem] as well as intergroup relationships...how members of different sociocultural groups view themselves and
see themselves in the world" (Sleeter & Grant, 1994, p. 98).

The Single-Group Studies approach was initially developed to fill gaps
in higher-education curricula and to provide support for those who feel
alienated from a predominantly White, male, heterosexual, able-bodied,
middle- and upper-middle-class environment. Many women's studies, ethnic studies, and gay studies departments still exist. The primary goal of each
is addressing the inequalities and imbalance of power experienced by peo-

ple in a specific "minority" group. By creating single-group studies departments, each group "hope[s] to broaden what is included in American culture so that the group in which they are interested is an important part, no
longer invisible or marginal" (Sleeter & Grant, 1994, pp. 123–124; for further discussion of marginalization, see the Epilogue). In a classroom of young
children, this approach would most likely take the form of a series of units
on specific groups. Sometimes the entire curriculum is devoted to one people. In Afrocentric schools the sole focus is to educate African American
children about the contributions of their ancestors and to provide a learning environment in which they can be empowered to feel strong and good
about themselves.

Sleeter and Grant's final two categories are the Multicultural Education
approach and the Education That Is Multicultural and Social Reconstructionist
approach. As the Multicultural Education approach is described at length in
the following pages, I won't go into it here. I do want, however, to identify
the significant differences between these two approaches and the others.
First, both are based on the belief that essential changes must be made in the
business-as-usual curriculum; these changes are not patched on but are necessary at its core. Second, great attention is paid to social-justice issues in
both of these approaches. The Education That Is Multicultural and Social
Reconstructionist is even stronger in this regard as it focuses on changing society so that power is shared equitably.

> [It] deals more directly than the other approaches with oppression and social
> structural inequality based on race, social class, gender, and disability.… The
> approach prepares future citizens to reconstruct society so that it better serves
> the interests of all groups of people and especially those who are of color,
> poor, female, gay and/or disabled. This approach is visionary. (pp. 209–210)

My own approach is drawn mostly from Multicultural Education and
Education That Is Multicultural and Social Reconstructionist, with elements
of Human Relations sprinkled throughout. Like other advocates of Multicultural Education, I "seek to reform the entire process of schooling for all
children" (Sleeter & Grant, 1994, p. 184). I also believe it is essential for educators to participate in social justice and institutional change work, as the
Education That Is Multicultural and Social Reconstructionist approach
encourages. From my perspective, both of these paths are "visionary"—moving forward to the future, believing that changing attitudes and institutions
is difficult but not impossible. I support pieces of the Human Relations
approach, particularly promoting self-esteem and dealing with stereotypes;
however, I don't believe the approach goes far enough in advocating change
in systems and practices.

As Sleeter and Grant acknowledge, multicultural education remains one of the critical issues facing educators today. At the center of the move toward multicultural education is the belief that this approach should permeate every level of the educational process. Sonia Nieto (1992) defines multicultural education as

> a process of comprehensive school reform and basic education for all students. It challenges and rejects racism and other forms of discrimination in schools and society and accepts and affirms the pluralism (ethnic, racial, linguistic, religious, economic, and gender, among others) that students, their communities, and teachers, represent. Multicultural education permeates the curriculum and instructional strategies used in schools, as well as the interaction among teachers, students and parents, and the very way that schools conceptualize the nature of teaching and learning.
>
> The seven basic characteristics of multicultural education are as follows:
> Multicultural education is *antiracist education.*
> Multicultural education is *basic education.*
> Multicultural education is *important for all students.*
> Multicultural education is *pervasive.*
> Multicultural education is *education for social justice.*
> Multicultural education is a *process.*
> Multicultural education is *critical pedagogy.* (p. 208)

The multicultural approach to education is not limited to buying appropriate culturally diverse classroom materials. The selection of staff in a racially diverse community also enhances multicultural education if they represent the diversity of the geographic area. Teacher participation in the interviewing and decision-making process contributes to the sharing of power among members of the school community. When each part of the educational institution addresses the issues of multicultural education and institutional racism, multicultural classroom materials will become fully effective.

In preschool classrooms, multicultural education has five primary goals:

1. To teach children to respect others' cultures and values as well as their own
2. To help all children learn to function successfully in a multicultural, multiracial society
3. To develop a positive self-concept in those children who are most affected by racism—children of color
4. To help all children experience in positive ways both their differences as culturally diverse people and their similarities as human beings
5. To allow children to experience people of diverse cultures working together as unique parts of a whole community

Young children who live in a multicultural community experience cultural diversity firsthand; it is part of their world. However, 3-, 4-, and 5-year-olds who live in monocultural settings may have difficulty imagining communities that are different from theirs. In such a monocultural community, the classroom can be both a familiar, comfortable setting for the children and a multicultural environment of experiences, pictures, music, and books pertaining to people of diverse cultural heritages. In a monocultural community, even more than in a multicultural community, it is crucial that teachers present differences among people as positive qualities. The foundation of respect for diversity will have been firmly laid as the children in a homogeneous community grow older and are better able to deal with specific information about various cultures.

I have chosen to address the issue of institutional racism through a book on multicultural curriculum development because I believe that "through guided classroom interaction, students' interracial attitudes may become more positive and accepting" (Chesler, 1971, p. 613). I have directed the book to teachers because they are the critical link between institutional racism, sexism, anti-Semitism, and heterosexism, among other issues— "isms"—and multicultural education. Teachers guide the interaction that Chesler describes. As a teacher, you can choose, from a range of levels, the extent of your involvement in multicultural education. No matter what level of involvement you choose, you will be guiding students toward the acceptance of diversity. Teachers who are very involved will design the entire classroom environment to reflect multiculturalism.

LANGUAGE AND NAMING

Another piece of our national and personal journey is the consistent effort to use language in a way that is respectful of others. In 1957, Lillian Smith, a White Southern woman, gave the commencement address at Atlanta University; the title of her speech was "The Winner Names the Age." In this country those of us who are White have historically had the privilege of *naming* events and people based on *our* perspective. American history books call the Battle of Little Bighorn "Custer's Last Stand" and speak of it as a massacre. If we were reading an account of that same conflict written by Native Americans, it would be labeled a glorious victory. Until very recently, history books presented slavery as an economic tool, a tragedy to be sure, but still something necessary to keep the Southern economic system, and hence the country's, profitable. Rarely are we given a picture of Black people's experience of slavery; even though much was written by people who were enslaved, those perspectives are only infrequently included in textbooks. One source of writing by people who were slaves is *Black Women in White America* by Gerda Lerner (1992) (see appendix A for further suggestions). Part of our journey as a nation is to come to grips with the issue of *naming*—to understand that in a just system all people have the opportunity to identify themselves *as they wish to be named.*

One of the hottest buttons in the country at this point is the issue of what people in various racial and gender groups are called. Often I hear, "Why can't those Black people [or Latinos or Asian Americans] decide what they want to be called? First it was *Negro* and then it was *Black* and now it's *African American*. Why should I keep up when they can't even decide themselves? This is too much trouble." Or, "I never know what females want to be called. What's wrong with *girl* or *lady*? What does it matter what people are called?" The people who seem in greatest consternation about this are those who are in the dominant groups—those of us who are White or those who are male. Because we have always been the namers, it is difficult to understand why naming is such an issue.

This is not about being "politically correct." It is about holding others' concerns in regard. My belief and my experience tell me that one of our primary challenges is to create genuine communities in which authentic and thoughtful communication can take place. If we want to be considerate of others, we will want to identify people as they want to be identified. The most important thing to remember is that, while individual terms may change over time, our desire for respectful conversation shouldn't. Our best clues come from listening to people as they talk about themselves. Wheelchair users do not refer to themselves as *wheelchair-bound*. Gender-integrated staffs work *hours*, not *man-hours;* they have *power*, not *manpower*. Children do not describe themselves as coming from *broken homes;* they come from *homes*. It is also fine to ask how people want to be identified. For example, I might say to someone, "I know that some people like to be called *Hispanic* and some prefer *Latino* or *Latina;* what is your preference?"

In the absence of personal knowledge of an individual's choices, here are some basic guidelines:

• *Black* and *African American* are the preferred terms, although there is a lot of conversation and disagreement among people who belong in this group. Some feel that, since their ancestors were brought from Africa to the United States against their will, they want to be addressed as *African American*. Others prefer to be called *Black* or *Black Americans*.

• *Latina/Latino* and *Hispanic* are generally the terms of choice for people whose cultural roots are in Spanish-speaking countries. *Latina* is female, *Latino* male. Some don't like *Hispanic* because they feel that it refers to people who are from Spain, not from Mexico or Central and Latin America. *Chicano* is still used among some second- and third-generation Mexican Americans. Often, the most appreciated term is country- or culture-specific: for example, *Puerto Ricano, Cubano, Mexicano,* and so on.

•   *Asian* or *Asian American,* not *Oriental,* are the names for those whose culture is Asian. Many Asian people would rather be identified as *Chinese* or *Chinese American* or *Japanese* or *Japanese American* so that their particular heritage is made clear. While many of us who are not Asian see all these groups as a mass of similar people, Asian cultures are very different from one another.

•   For those whose ancestors were the original inhabitants of our continent, *Native American, American Indian, Native Peoples,* or *indigenous peoples* are the preferred group terms. However, many Native Americans see themselves as members of their tribes, such as Hopi, Zuni, Cherokee, or Lakota.

•   Many people consider their religion or their religious heritage to be their main identification, such as some Jews (including some who seem assimilated), Black Muslims, and Jehovah's Witnesses. However, it is important to remember that, in our race-focused country, White Jews have privileges that Ethiopian Jews do not. While a Black person may see him- or herself as primarily a Jehovah's Witness, most people will see him or her first as Black.

•   While *White* is the term most frequently used for those whose skin is relatively fair, some prefer to be identified by their cultural roots and/or their American heritage. For example, many of those whose families came from Ireland identify themselves as *Irish Americans,* from Poland as *Polish Americans. Anglo* is used by many Latinos in the southwestern United States to refer to White people.

When writing about people of Eastern and Western European descent, I have chosen to capitalize *White.* I do so in order to give our group a sense of identity that we don't always recognize. While we are not always clear that we are White, people of color have no doubt of our racial identity.

•   *People of color* has been used for the last 10 or 15 years as a term for those who are not White. The term is not universally accepted, but it is the first choice among the alternatives. *Colored* is not the same as *people of color.* The former is an outdated term and is considered insulting to Black people. *Minority* is offensive to many people of color because in the world they are the majority; the term is still used, but it is gradually fading out.

•   *Biracial* and *multiracial,* not *mixed,* are the most appropriate designations for those whose parents and/or grandparents are racially different from one another. It is my experience that we who are not multiracial don't know how to categorize those who are. From older bi- and multiracial students I often hear comments such as: "I'm not White enough for my White friends and not Black enough for my Black friends"; "When I tried to join the Latino student group, they wouldn't let me because I look White"; and "I never know which box to check on forms. I'm not really Black, but part of me is. My mother is half African American and half Cherokee. My father was Irish Catholic and Jewish, with a little bit of Mexican too. I am a part of all those people." As the number of people in this group grows, we will, no doubt, learn to talk differently about the issue of race; it may eventually cease to be a useful notion. However, as long as we live in a country in which institutional racism (and other systemic discrimination) is firmly embedded and a person's life experience is so affected by who she or he is racially, the designation of one's race will continue to be essential.

THE JOURNEY THROUGH THIS BOOK

There are seven chapters, an epilogue, and two appendixes in this edition of *Diversity in the Classroom*. Chapter 1 has provided a context in which to place our continuing work as educators in the late 1990s and early 2000s. I have used the image of journeys to focus on the work that faces our country, our field, and each of us as we move toward genuine multiculturalism.

In Chapter 2, we look at how relationships with others, patterns of play, and problem-solving skills develop in young children. Increasingly, those of us in early childhood education are recognizing that culture greatly affects all aspects of a child's growth. If teachers are to be successful in enabling children's learning, they must gather and use cultural information about children without stereotyping them. Chapter 2 also includes discussions of identifying students' learning styles and the development of racial awareness and attitudes.

Before a teacher can create a curriculum that is genuinely multicultural, she or he must take the emotional risk of examining her or his behaviors and attitudes. Chapter 3 provides opportunities to begin (or continue) that process by pointing out necessary elements of self-examination: being willing to listen and change, remaining a life-long learner, and understanding the societal context in which we live and teach.

In Chapter 4, the central concern is building relationships with parents as preparation for talking about multicultural education. This discussion was intentionally placed before Chapter 5 on multiculturalism in the classroom to underscore the importance of parent involvement in the development of a curriculum. Too often, we as teachers decide what we are going to do with children and report that information to parents without taking their concerns into account. I believe it is essential to see parents as our partners in the development of their children's education; we must create ways to bring families into that process.

Chapters 6 and 7 offer concrete ideas about multicultural curricula. There is a unit plan on affirming cultural diversity in Chapter 6 and a discussion of creating multicultural learning areas in a preschool classroom in Chapter 7. At the end of Chapter 7 is a Classroom Environment Checklist which is useful in assessing strengths and weaknesses of a classroom. Some readers might have preferred my putting the concrete curriculum ideas at the beginning of this book; however, my intention is not to provide a collection of activities to do with children, but rather to give teachers the desire and skills to become more sophisticated in the process of teaching in a multicultural classroom. An aphorism I learned from a colleague at Tufts continues to guide my thoughts about helping teachers: "Give a person a fish, and she or he will eat for a day; teach a person to fish, and she or he will eat for a lifetime."

Appendixes A and B are annotated bibliographies of multicultural-related books for adults and children. Bibliographies are, by nature, subjective and incomplete; new books appear so quickly that such lists are almost obsolete by the time they are created. However, it seems important to provide a starting place simply because there are so many books on the market. Please use these lists as beginnings; add to them as you do your own reading.

A NOTE

A final thought as we journey further into *Diversity in the Classroom*: A journey is, by definition, a process; most of us are not comfortable in limbo. Particularly on journeys that take us into the core of ourselves or our institutions, we either wish we had not begun or want the trip to be over. Change does not come smoothly or quickly enough, and then it suddenly happens too fast.

Alice Walker, who has always been a teacher for me, talks about the profound concept of *revolutionary patience:* the patience that acknowledges the slowness of change, coupled with the understanding that to bring about revolutionary change takes constant, unrelenting work. She also wrestles with remaining comfortable with unanswered, and sometimes unanswerable, questions. Her directive to herself in the first stanza of her poem, *Reassurance* (1973), expresses our challenge as well.

REASSURANCE

I must love the questions
themselves
as Rilke said
like locked rooms
full of treasure
to which my blind
and groping key
does not yet fit.

Understanding
Child Development

The fields of early childhood education and child development are currently in an exciting, challenging, and in some ways uncomfortable time. We who identify ourselves as developmentalists are having to grapple with much tougher questions than we have in decades. We have come to this place in part because of the necessary reexamination of any theoretical perspective and in part because of the influx of children into the United States whose cultures and experiences are undeniably and dramatically different from those of the mainstream culture of this country. We must ask ourselves critical questions about what we really do know about child development. Which children did theorists have in mind when theory and practice were defined? Who was excluded? What role do culture, gender, class, and/or society play in a child's development and educational needs? What assumptions are we making about children as we design a "developmentally appropriate" curriculum? In his book *The Unschooled Mind* (1991), Howard Gardner addresses these questions. "According to our new and expanded understanding, mind exists equally within the skull, in the objects strewn about in the culture, and in the behaviors of other individuals with whom one interacts and from whom one learns" (p. 40). This being the case, we must view children through a much more encompassing theoretical lens.

At a workshop I was leading for children's center staffs in a large urban school district, I was asked if children who live with the daily danger of being shot or seeing someone killed go through the same stages of development as do children in safer environments. I didn't answer the question well. I think I mumbled that, even though their *experiences* were different, the order of their developmental stages was the same. I wish I had said, "I (and we in early childhood education and development) don't know for sure." What is the cognitive and emotional effect of living with a level of violence that many of us cannot, and do not want to, imagine? How does the uncertainty of belonging to a homeless family alter a child's development? What about the children who live at an inhuman level of poverty? Is the title of Alex Kotlowitz's book about two boys growing up in housing projects in Chicago, *There Are No Children Here* (1991), an apt description? I don't know. What I do know is that we in this country and, of course, in the world, will be affected by a generation of children who have grown up in war zones. (For more information on the resiliency of children, see Dugan & Coles, 1989; Garmezy, 1991; and Rutter, 1990.) Whether those wars were in Serbia, Rwanda, Chicago, or Belfast, the lives of these children have been significantly different from those most of the developmental theorists originally studied.

Teachers and caregivers are increasingly forced to reexamine long-held ideas about how children learn, what affects their growth and development, and how to create learning environments in which *all* children can thrive. We can no longer talk about the development of "the preschool child" with any assuredness that we are talking about any children other than the White middle-class ones on whose development the theories were based. Rather, we must recognize "the child's embeddedness in a family, a community, a culture, and a society" (New & Mallory, 1994, p. 8). When assessing the child's development, we must focus on the specific children about whom we are speaking. The point is *not* to stereotype children with preconceptions such as "This is a girl so we should not expect her to be good at math." Instead, the challenge is to recognize the messages the child is getting in her life that affect her ability to think mathematically and assess her developmental stage with that information in mind.

These ideas have been part of our knowledge base for decades. Integral to Shapiro and Biber's (1972) developmental–*interaction* theory (italics mine) is the assumption that an individual child's developmental needs must be assessed *in relation to* that child's cultural and social experience. Barbara Bowman and Frances Stott (1994) of the Erikson Institute acknowledge that there are some aspects of development that are similar across cultures, such as "establishing mutually satisfying social relationships, organizing and integrating perceptions, learning language, developing category systems, thinking, imagining, and creating" (p. 120). At the same time, there is a shift occurring. The fields of early childhood education and child development are reaching toward a new level of understanding that broadens analysis from the individual to the cultural context. Bowman and Stott go on to say that "developmental milestones

... take on their meaning only in the context of social life" (p. 120). Gardner (1991) makes clear that it is not *whether* all normal children develop the ability to understand and use symbols—that is a given. It is *how* they do it and what symbols they acquire that is affected by their culture.

For purposes of this book, *culture* will be defined as a people's way of doing things, a system of rules for making meaning of the universe. Our values and belief systems, ways of thinking, acting, and responding, grow out of this set of rules and greatly influence our behavior. "How children learn to organize their environment, which language they learn to speak, how they occupy their leisure time—all have significance for the kinds of problems they will solve and the strategies they will use to do so" (Bowman & Stott, 1994, p. 121).

When teachers take the interaction of culture and development seriously, their responsibilities are heightened. Bowman and Stott, Yonemura (1986), and others remind us that two of a teacher's key roles are those of inquirer and learner. As we work to understand the importance of family, community, culture, and society in each child's development, each teacher's challenge is to move with a curious mind toward new perspectives rather than backing away from them.

Generally speaking, young children are concerned with finding out who they are and what they can do. As they develop, children move out from themselves and away from their total involvement with their own growth. They move toward acceptance of their roles in a society of individuals who work for other people's well-being in addition to their own. Facilitating their process of moving from self-involvement to caring about and taking responsibility for others is part of a teacher's job as she or he works with children and their parents. One way of facilitating the process is by adopting a multicultural approach when designing a learning environment for young children.

As noted in Chapter 1, the child-development framework on which this book is based reflects a combination of philosophies: the developmental–interaction point of view (Biber, 1977; Biber, Shapiro, & Wickens, 1971; Shapiro & Biber, 1972), a philosophy of education for human relations (Taba, 1955), and the culture-as-context perspectives of Cole and Cole (1993), Lisa Delpit (1986), Howard Gardner (1991), and Lev Vygotsky (1978). Essential to all of these philosophies is the goal of helping children grow into competent and caring adults involved in creating a world in which all of us live interdependently.

Biber et al. (1971) describe the developmental–interaction theory as follows:

> *Developmental* refers to the emphasis on identifiable patterns of growth and modes of experiencing and responding associated with increasing chronological age. *Interaction* refers to the emphasis on the individual's interaction

with the environment. It indicates the central importance of the child's inter-action with other people, adults and children, as well as with material objects of the environment; it refers also to the interaction between cognitive and affective spheres of development. It is a formulation which places compara-ble stress on the nature of the environment and on the patterns of the responding child, assuming an environment which provides maximum opportunity for engagement. (p. 6)

Taba's (1955) philosophy of education emphasizes the importance of counteracting influences that "cultivate" children's ethnocentricity. She alerts teachers to the necessity of developing in students an awareness of the pos-itive aspects of cultural diversity:

The development of a cosmopolitan sensitivity and of a capacity to respond to human problems, values and feelings is a central task in education for human relations. Each individual grows up in a somewhat limiting cultural shell by virtue of the fact that the immediate primary groups in which a grow-ing person is socialized are culturally unique. While living in today's world requires a broad orientation to life, some American communities are still bounded by qualifications regarding race, economic status, and ethnic ori-gin. These differences tend to be maintained by separation of residence areas, by separate patterns of social association, and, therefore, by different life experiences. These experiences in the hemmed in cultural climates tend to cultivate ethnocentricity, or a tendency to interpret all other persons' behavior values, and motivations in terms of one's own values. (p. 100)

Cole and Cole's, Gardner's, and Vygotsky's perspectives will be described in the following pages. Chapter 2 explores three topics at length: the develop-ment of preschool children; how learning styles, culture, and ethnicity affect behavior; and, finally, how racial awareness and racial attitudes develop.

PRESCHOOL CHILDREN

In the preschool years, a great many exciting changes take place in the child. Between the ages of $2\frac{1}{2}$ and 5, children change vastly in terms of their rela-tionships with other people, their patterns of play, and their approaches to problem solving. While young preschool children are like toddlers in many ways, many older preschool children are articulate and skilled, and have a strong sense of self. Obviously, culture and environment affect how children see themselves, as well as how they develop skills and communication. Preschool teachers who are able to apply their knowledge about the different ways that children learn as well as about the changes that occur in the preschool years are better able to create a curriculum that is appropriate for each child.

Relationships with Other People

In some cultures, very young children relate primarily to members of their immediate families. For infants and toddlers in those cultures, people outside the family seem to be of little importance. In other communities and cultures, many people are involved in raising children. The African expression "It takes a village to raise a child" expresses a fundamentally different way of thinking about who is involved in raising children from the notion of a nuclear family's meeting all of a child's needs.

For children who have spent their first years in a relatively contained environment, the preschool years bring a real shift in experience as the children's circles of significant people grow wider. If a preschool-age child is in a nursery school or day-care center, she or he necessarily comes in contact with at least one additional important adult, the teacher, and also becomes part of a larger group of peers. Gradually the child who has had limited involvement with a variety of significant people grows comfortable with the new group of people, although the adjustment for her or him may be more difficult than it is for children raised in a broader community.

The degree to which individual preschool children are viewed as "egocentric" depends on the values and beliefs of the culture in which a child is raised, the behavioral norms and expectations of the adults who are involved with the child, and the child's particular personality. Swiss psychologist Jean Piaget believed that preschool children are, by definition, cognitively and affectively egocentric. For him, egocentrism in young children refers not to doing something for one's own benefit, but rather to a child's total inability to see another point of view. In the past few years, however, many studies have been done that call into question the extent to which Piaget's theories are applicable to *all* children (see Cole & Cole, 1993, for a discussion of recent research). Some theorists, such as Erica Burman (1994), remind us that the very definitions of "children and childhood are *constructed*; we therefore have to study not only 'the child,' but also the context (that is, the interpersonal, cultural, historical and political situation) that produces her" (p. 6). In most cases, young children see the world from their particular perspectives and have less understanding than adults do that there are other views to be considered.

Clearly, then, one shouldn't expect young children necessarily to be able to transcend themselves in order to see that each is only one of many children in a classroom. Actions that may seem selfish or self-centered are often the children's acting out of their views of the world. Therefore, one of the crucial jobs for adults involved with young children is helping them develop sympathy and empathy. Children, as they become less centered on themselves, begin to sympathize with their peers. In situations in which they themselves are not threatened, toddlers are capable of showing sympathetic behavior toward their immediate families, but it is not until the preschool years that many children begin to be authentically concerned for and sympathetic to others' needs (Cole & Cole, 1993).

Egocentrism is a predictable stage of development for young children, and, as Stone and Church (1973) noted, "egocentrism provides the foundation for *ethnocentrism,* taking for granted the ways of behaving, the values and the ideas of the people among whom one grows up" (p. 90). The most troubling aspect of ethnocentrism is the belief that one's own ethnic group or race is superior to all others, so that part of being ethnocentric is a sense of moral righteousness, that the values and rules of one's group are those by which everyone should live. It is interesting to note that, while most children seem to outgrow their egocentrism or learn to mask it, their ethnocentrism remains. One explanation for this phenomenon is that egocentrism is a quality that many cultures reject, including much of middle-class American culture. There are all sorts of maxims encouraging children to be less egocentric. The Golden Rule and the saying "Share and share alike," for example, warn children that they must give up their childish, selfish ways. Ethnocentrism, however, is firmly rooted in our culture. Many mainstream Americans expect everyone to speak English and to adhere to our culture's rules. As a society, we assume that everyone shares "our" values and, if not, that they should. The anti-immigrant sentiment and the English-as-the-only-language referendums are examples of the ways in which ethnocentrism is exhibited in this country.

A multicultural classroom environment is one way to begin to address ethnocentrism. Offering a variety of ways for children to learn and reinforcing the importance of each child's own cultural experience allow children to see that each of their particular ways of doing things is one of many. With positive early experiences in multicultural education, children can be helped to move from egocentrism to an understanding and appreciation of ethnic diversity rather than being bound by an ethnocentric perspective.

Patterns of Play

Play is part of every child's growth process; it has the odd distinction of being a virtually universal activity and at the same time an extremely culturally specific one. Cultural models of development identify

> three interacting layers of environmental influence on play: (1) physical and social aspects of children's immediate settings; (2) historical influences that affect the way adults (and children) conceptualize play; and (3) cultural and ideological beliefs relative to the meaning of play for subgroups of children. (Roopnarine & Johnson, 1994, pp. 4–5)

A brief exploration of these influences might be helpful in understanding Roopnarine and Johnson's point. The physical environment has great impact on how children play. Children who grow up in rural Montana, for example, have a very different sense of space in which to play than those who grow up in Brooklyn, New York—it is far more difficult to build a fort on Flatbush Avenue than it is on a Montana ranch. A child's socioeconomic status obviously affects the materials with which she or he plays. For those who grow up in wealthy families, computers are likely to be available for children's enjoyment from a very early age; for most poor children, access to expensive learning materials simply doesn't exist. Choices of what to play, when to play, and where to play are related to the environment and to socioeconomic class. Poor children have far fewer choices.

Adult (and thus children's) notions of play are often affected by the role that play has historically had in the culture. In Western European cultures, play occurs during leisure time and is seen as the opposite of work. In some Vietnamese households, whether in Vietnam or in the United States, very young children work in the families' businesses. Play is something that happens after work is done. The same holds true for children who grow up on farms or ranches. In other cultures, like some Native American ones, play and work are more intertwined as children's play often mimics the work an adult is doing. In cultures that have been involved in conflict for long periods of time, children's play is filled with reenactments of war games—children in Northern Ireland play Catholics versus Protestants, while those in inner-city projects might act out dodging bullets as they walk to school.

Ideology about play differs across cultures. For some, play is seen as a creative process—a time for children to be left to their own devices to pretend to be other people or to imagine different realities. For others, play consists of a series of structured lessons—piano, swimming, horseback riding, tennis. Obviously, the economic status of the adults in the family has impact on a child's access to such lessons. We live in a period (and in a country) in which watching television or playing video games consumes a large portion of children's nonschool time and is viewed as play. For some, reading or story-telling are primary ways of using leisure. In other groups, much of play focuses on active involvement with other people.

Finally, the materials that children use in play are closely tied to their cultural, experiential, and economic environment. For example, for children who grow up in a family that hunts, whether in Africa or Texas, guns and other hunting tools are a natural material for play. (In many American families, the owning of guns is gender-related; boys are given guns so they can learn to be "men"; girls are given dolls to practice being "mommies.") Children who grow up in wealthier families might play dress-up with their parents' old clothes; for many poorer children, simply having one pair of shoes for each family member at the same time is a luxury. Thus it is necessary for teachers and caregivers to consider that play and play materials take on very different significance in each individual's context. In many child-care centers, for example, making necklaces out of macaroni is a favorite activity. Sometimes the macaroni is painted first, sometimes dusted with glitter, sometimes glued together before stringing. For well-fed, middle-class American children, that may seem a fine way to practice manual dexterity. For children whose families don't have enough to eat, however, using food as a play material takes on quite different meaning. Even for children who, themselves, have plenty of food but whose families are conscious that there are many hungry children in the world, the activity has a confusing feel to it.

Two theorists, Jean Piaget and Lev Vygotsky, have dominated the field of psychological research on play in the last 50 to 60 years. It is helpful to look very briefly at their respective thoughts on the role that play has in the development of children. These theories are reference points for the teacher as she or he creates a play environment for children. Essentially, Piaget believed that children's play evolves from practice play to symbolic play to play with rules.

> Piaget asserts that the development of play progresses from purely individual processes and idiosyncratic private symbols to social play and collective symbolism. It derives from the child's mental structure, so that it can only be explained by that structure. (Nicolopoulou, 1991, p. 132)

In other words, play is primarily carried out as part of an *individual* child's developmental growth. Even when playing with others, the impetus is that of an individual assimilating and accommodating new information.

Vygotsky, on the other hand, believes that the child's primary purpose for play is not individual but social. For Vygotsky, play

> typically involves more than one child; and the themes, stories, or roles that play episodes enact express the children's understanding and appropriation of the sociocultural materials of their society.... Vygotsky's emphasis on the essentially social character of play accords with the main thrust of his larger psychological theory, which gives a key role to culture, and to its transmission through social interaction and communication, in the formation of the mind. (Nicolopoulou, 1991, p. 134)

Probably both theorists would agree that for preschool children play serves many purposes: it is a vehicle through which an enormous amount of learning takes place; it offers the opportunity to practice skills; it is a way to make social connections; and it helps children make sense of the world. Children also use play to explore unknown situations. Jerome Bruner (1976) stresses that through play children are given "an excellent opportunity to try combinations of behavior that would, under functional pressure, never be tried" (p. 38). Providing a psychologically safe environment for preschoolers in which they can

practice new roles and solutions without the threat of the consequences that
may occur in non-play situations supports the children's growth and learning.

Dramatic play is a critical activity for preschool children. Through it a
child is able to try on new roles or solve problems in a variety of ways. In different cultures and contexts, dramatic play focuses on various aspects of a
child's life. For example, a child's play may involve assuming the role of the
powerful parent who must discipline a disobedient child. Or it might provide an opportunity for a child who has newly immigrated to the United
States to try on what are for her or him extremely odd (foreign) behaviors.
Through the medium of dramatic play a child can experience another child's
view of the world. In it the child also experiences the positive effects of coop-
erating with other children without risking her or his egocentric world view.
Thus teachers who plan their classroom activities to support both spontaneous play and a variety of social interactions help children learn to coordinate
their needs with those of others. In general, play can help children grow out
of their egocentric and ethnocentric pictures of the world.

Problem Solving

Preschool children tend to take things at face value and are inclined to
believe what they see. Many are not yet able to imagine alternative solutions
to situations or problems, and some are just beginning to practice seeing

things from varying perspectives. This is another aspect of a young child's ego-centricity and is true in both the cognitive and affective spheres of development. For example, in the cognitive domain many young children are not able to reverse operations (Cole & Cole, 1993). That is, they are not able to retrace their steps. When a 3-year-old block builder is told it is time to clean up, she or he will probably do one of two things: either remove the first block used, which is, of course, at the bottom, or knock the whole building down. Many young builders are not able to see the alternative solution of disassembling the building by first removing the last block used.

Often young children also do what Piaget has labeled "transductive thinking." That is, children move from one specific piece of information to another without forming generalizations (Cole & Cole, 1993). Further, many young children are able to concentrate on only one attribute of an object at a time. Thus preschool children frequently are unable to get an overall view of the world. Toward the end of the preschool years children begin to organize language and thought processes and are able to transcend themselves and the here and now. As thought processes grow more complex, problem-solving skills become more logical.

Similarly, in the affective domain, if two young children want the same toy, often the only solution either of them can imagine is egocentric. While each child may believe that she or he should have the toy, culture often affects how the situation is addressed. In some cultures, for example, if the struggle is between an older child and a younger child, the older one automatically gets the toy. In other cultures, the opposite is true. In some subgroups, if one of the children involved is a boy and the other a girl, the toy in question automatically goes to the boy. The way conflict is handled in general is culturally affected. Some families allow no conflict; others see it as a way to increase logical thinking skills. Still others consider conflict a normal and necessary part of daily life. Because teachers play an important role in offering various solutions to children, it is vital that they are clear about the children's families' cultural rules as well as their own inherent cultural biases about fairness, conflict, sharing, and methods of problem solving. A teacher who is of the let-them-work-it-out-on-their-own school, for example, will respond very differently to a struggle over a toy than the one who unconsciously believes that a girl should show "good manners" and share her toys with others.

Preschool children are not always able to differentiate between fantasy and reality, which makes solving problems even more complicated than it might otherwise be. For example, if you have one cookie and two children want it, the act of breaking it in half to share it often reduces both children to tears. While the reality is that each child has half of the original cookie, the belief is that neither child has anything because it is now broken and not the object it was. For many young children, the people on television seem as real to them as the people in a store; dreams are as real as events that occur when they are awake. Many commonplace activities seem like magic to preschool children; electric lights come on mysteriously, just as cars are run by unseen powers. As children get older, they become increasingly concerned with determining what is fantasy and what is reality. Adults play a vital role as reality agents for preschool children when they offer pictures of what is actual; children are then better able to apply their skills in creating solutions for what is real, not for what they fear is true.

Part of preschool children's charm lies in their constant change and growth. During these years most grow from being very egocentric to caring for and sympathizing with other people. Their frequent inability to differentiate between fantasy and reality enables them to enjoy the world of make-believe and at the same time keeps them very vulnerable. Although their lack of problem-solving skills is frequently frustrating both to them and to adults around them, the children's excitement at exploring new knowledge and abilities eases the frustrations. In essence, rapid shifts in temperament and behavior and continually varying responses to environment characterize preschool children.

LEARNING STYLES

Historically, educators have acted as if there were a set body of knowledge to learn (multiplication tables in third grade, populations and capitals of each of the 50 states in fourth) and a set way for every child to learn. Even our classrooms are traditionally set up in similar ways in schools across the country: each child has an individual desk (usually designed for right-handed children), the desks are placed in rows, all facing the front of the room where the fount of knowledge, the teacher, stands. Most information is presented either verbally or in books. Certainly, over the years, early childhood education has made much-needed changes in the classroom environment. Now many classrooms are designed with learning centers in which several activities are taking place at the same time. Children often have the opportunity to make choices about what they want to do, thereby enhancing their ability to make decisions, and they are able to work in groups. But there continue to be basic assumptions made about the way children learn; too often, teachers still act as if there is a "right" answer to everything and the task of educators is to pass on to others in defined ways what they themselves learned.

Howard Gardner (1991) has suggested another way of looking at how we learn that is much more in keeping with the need to provide learning opportunities for children who are very different from one another. He believes that

> all human beings are capable of at least seven different ways of knowing the world…through language, logical–mathematical analysis, spatial represen-

tation, musical thinking, the use of the body to solve problems or to make things, an understanding of other individuals, and an understanding of ourselves. (p. 12)

Gardner believes that we differ in the ways that we use each of those intelligences to solve problems, assess situations, learn new information, and carry out tasks. Further, each of us has some intelligences that are stronger than others, a style of learning that we prefer to others. We grapple with problems in a variety of ways; we ask different questions, and we ask questions differently. Some of us prefer to learn by listening to information being discussed. Others seek information from books. Still others approach an experience by observing or attempting the actual thing to be learned. There is not a right way or a wrong way—there are different ways. The most important thing to remember is that children are individuals with personal styles of learning. By helping students discover their particular learning styles and the kinds of intelligence which are their strongest, you, as a teacher, can help them learn more efficiently and effectively.

Considering Cultural Differences

There is both empirical and common-sense evidence that learning styles are greatly affected by culture. By looking at a behavior and the very different ways in which that behavior is responded to, we know that cultural context affects meaning. In some cultures, a girl begins to cry and the adults around her comfort her and say, "There, there." A boy does the very same thing and the adults say, "Stop crying. Big boys don't cry." The cultural messages are clear, and each child is likely to develop learning patterns that take this reality into consideration. A child is born into a culture where "children are seen but not heard." When he talks loudly and interrupts adults, he is punished for being disrespectful. Had he been born into a culture in which children are supposed to interact with others and are rewarded for verbal ability and energy, the behavior would be viewed differently. In sum, what the children would have learned would have been very different, even though the behaviors were the same.

Suppose two children from different cultural backgrounds begin preschool on the same day. One has been praised since infancy for her willingness to explore the unknown and to try new things. The other has been taught that one should never touch anything that belongs to someone else without being invited to do so. As the two girls come into the school, the first rushes to try all the new materials. She talks to the children and to the teacher, asking questions about how everything works. The other little girl stays very close to her big brother, who has brought her to school. She doesn't speak to the teachers, even when spoken to, and she touches nothing. Unless the teachers are careful, their personal, often unconscious, assumptions about how children should move into new situations may well get in the way of seeing what is really going on with each child. As Bowman and Stott (1994) tell us, "Cultural differences can lead teachers to misunderstand children, to assess incorrectly their developmental competence, and to plan incorrectly for their educational achievement" (p. 121). In a heterogeneous classroom teachers must also manage the tension of different cultural expectations. Many Asian families, for example, want their children to learn to respect authority, while many European American middle-class parents value fostering children's independence and critical thinking. Teachers in these situations must respond to the parents' desires for their children's growth and, at the same time, create an environment in which all children feel treated fairly.

Lest we think that cultural differences always refer to non-American, non-White groups, let me tell you a story about my own cultural experience. I was raised in a strong Southern culture by a mother who had definite opinions about what was proper behavior and what was not. In her mind, it was *not* appropriate for a young Southern lady to romp around outside, or, in fact, to do adventuresome physical things anywhere. At boarding school when I was asked in 10th grade to turn a cartwheel in gym class, I tried but fell and tore my knee cartilage. It was the first cartwheel I had ever tried to do. The gym teacher could have identified me as developmentally or physically delayed or abnormal or as too chubby. Each was a possibility. However, unless she had consciously thought about, read about, and considered my cultural history, she would have missed a major element of my story. "Proper" young Southern ladies (by my mother's definition) didn't do cartwheels or climb trees. And, if I was going to please my mother, I had to spend my time playing with dolls rather than romping outside. I had no experience in developing myself physically and certainly no cultural support to do so. How we learn and what we learn are most definitely affected by our cultural messages.

Gathering and Using Cultural Information Without Stereotyping

In order to enable children to learn in the ways that make most sense to them as individuals, you, as a teacher, need to be aware of and knowledgeable about each child's cultural and ethnic background and then be able to use that cultural information as one piece of the puzzle that is the child. The complicated part of this process is that there is, indeed, a fine line between awareness of the potential effects of culture and ethnicity on learning styles and expecting a child of a particular ethnic group to behave in a particular way—in other words, stereotyping. Ideally, you do not view any child as a representative of her or his cultural or ethnic group but respond to each one as an individual for whom culture or ethnicity is merely one aspect of her or his personality.

There are lots of ways you can gather information about a child's cultural and ethnic heritage. Obviously, one of the best sources of information is the child's family, though it is important that you not force the parents to assume the role of your educator if the parents are not comfortable being that. There are books, movies, and newspaper and magazine articles that provide information. Also, if there are a large number of people in the community who share this child's background, chances are good that there are organizations and associations with which you could talk. Churches, mosques, synagogues, and other places of worship provide opportunities to experience an aspect of someone's culture. In short, the first part of understanding a child's experience is to learn as much as you possibly can of that child's heritage.

The second part is harder. As you are pulling information together, it is essential to remember that cultural information only provides clues, not concrete data, about particular people; and so, even though you have information about a specific culture or ethnic group, it won't necessarily apply to all the people in that group. One of the ways to find out how (and if) cultural information applies to a specific child is by observing. The teacher tries to observe each child without expectations based on race, ethnicity, gender, or life experience, and uses the information gained through this observation to design appropriate learning experiences for the child.

Learning to observe children objectively is difficult. A critical ingredient of objective observation is an awareness of the assumptions one brings to the observational process. Just as the examination of one's attitudes about race, gender, physical abilities, and sexual orientation are essential prior to setting up a multicultural classroom environment, so an exploration of the suppositions and expectations fostered by one's own cultural heritage is important before beginning to observe children. Often, our cultural biases are so much a part of the way we view the world that we have no idea that our attitudes are affecting our assessment of a child. (See the exercise on cultural biases in Chapter 3, Figure 3.3, for a clearer understanding of how our own assumptions affect the ways we see the world.) For instance, if you come from a culture that values learning by example, you might find it difficult to observe objectively a child who learns by actively exploring learning materials; you might unconsciously feel that the child is making a mess. Or if you grew up in a family in which your mother was a grocery store checker and your father was a roofer, you might resent an upper-middle-class family in which both parents are members of professions and hire other people to care for their children, mow their lawns, and scrub their floors. Chances are good that you will have to work very hard to report about the child objectively and not see her or him as spoiled and overly privileged. If you are aware of your own biases, objective observation will be far easier. That doesn't mean that we have to like what we see, but it does mean that we need to see what is going on as clearly as possible. (For more information about observation in general, see Cohen, Stern, & Ballaban, 1983; Irwin & Bushnell, 1980; and Nicholson & Shipstead, 1994.)

Before considering specific cultural information and ways to use that information without falling into the trap of stereotyping, let's look at what we mean by *cultural information* and what stereotypes are and how we go about using them. *Cultural information* is data about a group of people who share a common cultural heritage or background. While the information applies to the group as a whole, it does not necessarily apply to each individual in that group. For example: one of the cultures in the United States is a male culture. (If you are not clear about what the "male culture" is, think of the interactive behaviors of men on sports teams.) One of the rules of that culture is that men cannot show emotions in the same ways that women are allowed to, that they should be brave, tough, "masculine." While the rules for the male culture vary somewhat across race, class, or ethnic lines, there are still rules, values, and behaviors that are apt to be reinforced in male children quite different from those that are part of the female culture in this country.

A *stereotype* is a standardized picture of an object or person, created without taking the whole object or person into account. It is a lazy way of thinking, a shortcut. For example, there are some similar attributes among many Native American people—a range of skin colors, hair textures, and, for those raised in tribal cultures, some shared historical and cultural heritage. There are also vast differences. Stereotyping occurs when we *expect* or *assume* that a Native American who is a parent of a new child in your classroom will have the same needs, concerns, and behaviors as the Native American parent who was part of the classroom community last year. The common stereotype of Native Americans in the United States today is that they are spiritual, connected to and concerned about the earth, and live on reservations. While statistically the chances are good that a Native American child in your classroom has some ancestors who lived on a reservation, it would be unwise to assume that an individual child's experience has been affected by reservation life. Similarly, while there is cultural information about the Hopi or Cherokee as a group in terms of religious practices, we don't know about every individual Hopi's spiritual beliefs. The lazy thinking comes when we presume to know something about an individual based on something we have heard or learned about that person's group.

What follows is information that speaks to some of the most obvious ways that cultures vary one from another and their possible effects on learning: ways of interacting with authority figures, perceptions of time, displays of emotion, styles of communication. Such information might be used to advise a teacher's behavior.

• In many Asian, Black, Latino, and Native American cultures children are taught that making eye contact with an adult is disrespectful, while in many White middle-class cultures, looking an authority figure in the eye signifies honor and truthfulness. Because many Western European American teachers value eye contact and relate it to the ability to interact well with people, the refusal to make eye contact may be viewed as a behavior to be corrected. As is often the case when we are talking about cultural differences, from a truly objective stance there is no right or wrong, just a difference. But, because we are products of our own culture or cultures, unless we have done some thinking about our personal cultural biases, the differences are experienced as having more or less value. Being reprimanded for looking away when talking with a teacher may be very confusing for an Hispanic, Asian, or Native American child. The child may have been taught at home to avert her or his eyes when being addressed by an elder, yet at school the teacher, an important elder, is giving the child a very different message about preferred and appropriate behavior. Your task is to be aware of this cultural information and then *to check if that is what is being played out.* Cultural messages are one possible reason for the child's not looking the teacher in the eye. Other options are that the child is sick, angry, visually impaired, distracted, or frightened. If a teacher is aware of this part of a child's cultural training, however, she or he will be better able to read the behavior.

• The ways in which new information is processed differ from culture to culture. Some children are taught new skills and information by observing an activity closely for a long period of time. For example, Vera John (1972) suggests that many Navajo children have highly developed visual discrimination and fine motor skills and learn to absorb the world through sight and touch. That is the model for learning that many have been taught or experienced; they learn best by observing an activity for a long time before trying to do it themselves. For some Navajo children, then, teaching strategies that emphasize demonstration and materials that invite active manipulation are most appropriate to the child's already developed learning strategy. Your verbal direction to "match the blocks of the same color" may not be as successful as a demonstration of matching by you or a classmate.

• The child's perception of time is also relevant to learning styles (Hovey, 1975). Cultural groups experience time in different ways. For example, being "on time" in Western European cultures means arriving at a designated place when the hands of the clock say that a specific time has arrived. In other cultures, being "on time" means getting to an appointment when all of the things that needed to be done before that appointment have been completed. Instead of being measured in discrete hour and minute segments, time is measured by how long it takes to complete a task. In Sioux culture, there is no word for "time" or for "late" or for "waiting." In fact, clocks are not items one would find in traditional Sioux homes (Hall, 1959). (For fascinating discussions of time and other cultural phenomena, see Hall, 1959, 1966.) Werner, Bierman, and French (1971) suggest that, because time means so many things to different cultures, some children do poorly on performance tests that are based on a White middle-class understanding of time as minutes and hours. Pacing activities on individual children's bases and giving advance notice of transitions so that children will have the chance to reorient their internal clock mechanisms are two ways to accommodate each child's perception of time.

• The ways in which we display emotion are definitely affected by cultural messages. For some groups, displaying any emotion in public is forbidden; for others, emotion is an essential part of communication. Many Asian children are taught to value silence and to avoid overt displays of emotion (Kuroiwa, 1975). For some teachers who are more comfortable with spontaneous, verbal expression of emotion, the Asian child may seem shy and withdrawn. In order to allow for the child's preference of not expressing emotion openly, you will want to provide a variety of avenues for the expression of feelings. Mime, charades, creative movement, and dramatic play can all serve as vehicles through which a child can be expressive in ways that are most comfortable for her or him.

• Obviously, all communication is culturally bound. The very means of communicating (writing, the use of the telephone, person-to-person interaction) are affected by unwritten cultural rules and, in turn, influence how we learn. One of the greatest sources of miscommunication among people who are culturally different from one another is communication *style*. In *Black and White Styles in Conflict*, Thomas Kochman (1981) graphically portrays what he identifies as the different communication styles that Whites and Blacks have:

> Black presentations are emotionally intense, dynamic, and demonstrative; white presentations are more modest and emotionally restrained.... Where whites use the relatively detached and unemotional *discussion* mode to engage an issue, blacks use the more emotionally intense and involving mode of *argument*. (p. 106)

While there is a real danger of stereotyping Whites and Blacks when we use this information, it is too important to leave out of the discussion. If a child is used to learning in a manner that is infused with emotion, a presentation of information that is flat and fact-filled is not likely to engage her or him. On the other hand, if a child is used to getting information in a logical, sequential, unemotional manner, a lively presentation may seem overwhelming. Further, if a child experiences as anger the strong emotion displayed by a speaker when the speaker is merely emotionally involved, the communication is distorted and learning is hampered. Obviously, in order to provide for a variety of ways of learning, a teacher must vary her or his styles of teaching to be most effective.

Culture and ethnicity have deep impact on our learning styles. The examples cited here are illustrative, rather than comprehensive or conclusive. Teachers who wish to understand the learning styles of children in multi-ethnic classes can frequently get useful clues by studying their cultures. Some sources for particular cultures are cited in Appendix A. But culture and ethnicity are obviously not the sole determinants of learning style; it is essential that teachers not make assumptions about a child's learning style based solely on the child's cultural heritage. Not all Asian American children learn to refrain from verbal expression of emotion; not all Navajo children learn most readily through demonstration; and not all Latino children look away when speaking with adults. Your responsibility is to determine the preferred learning style of each child in the classroom and to plan for that child's school experience accordingly.

Identifying Learning Styles

The first step in identifying a child's learning style is to observe her or his various ways of interacting in a learning environment. The goal is to determine as accurately as possible what work habits a child uses in her or his most successful learning encounters. Information from experiences that are frustrating to a child might tell you as much as the ones that seem to go without struggle. For example, if a child seems to be unable to engage in productive activity after verbal directions have been given, you can look to see if there is a pattern of inability to respond to learning that emphasizes listening. If so, you can then try using pictorial or written directions, demonstrating a particular procedure for the child, or encouraging the child to observe other children engaged in the activity. You might also want to check to see if the child has a hearing problem.

Once patterns are identified, you should try to determine how much of a child's learning style may be connected with her or his culture and how much is due to the child's individual personality. Wilma Longstreet (1978) has outlined a format for considering cultural influences on learning style that is useful for teachers who are attempting to address differences in learning style. She considers both the factors that affect a child's predisposition to learn and the behavioral patterns that affect how learning takes place.

According to Longstreet, there are three factors that influence a child's predisposition to learning: classroom atmosphere, relevance of information, and appropriateness of materials. The best atmosphere for learning differs from one child to another. Riessman (1966) suggests that we too often expect

learning to take place only in a particularly quiet atmosphere: "Strangely enough, some people do their best studying in a noisy place, or with certain sounds such as music or even traffic in the background" (p. 16). If a child has a large family and is accustomed to a lot of noise, an exceedingly quiet classroom might make working difficult. If, on the other hand, the child's home environment is very quiet, the child may have trouble concentrating while other children are moving about or talking to one another.

Obviously, then, cultural traits are not the only variables to be taken into account when assessing the kind of learning environment a child needs. It is important as well to consider messages the child has received early in life about noise, neatness, and discipline when working. (Of course, one's perceptions of "noise," "neatness," and "discipline" are also related to cultural beliefs and values.) In order to accommodate the various needs of the children, teachers should provide different types of learning environments within the classroom. There should be quiet places in the room for children whose tolerance of noise is low and more open spaces for children who work well with more stimuli. For children who seem to need a working space that is always theirs, specific desks or table spaces could be set aside. The children for whom a specific space does not appear to be necessary can work in various parts of the room as their tasks require.

The relevance of the curricular material to the child's concerns partially determines how children respond to its presentation. Because of their narrow frames of reference, young children are most comfortable with content areas that are somewhat familiar to them. They pay better attention to topics that have some connection to their experience. For example, stories that have as the main characters White families in suburban or rural settings are simply not relevant to children of color in an urban, integrated school. I remember trying to convince a group of 3-year-olds in a day-care center in Brooklyn, New York, that milk comes from cows. It was impossible. They knew milk came in cartons from stores because they had seen it. To ease children from materials with which they are familiar to ones that reflect experiences different from theirs, it is helpful to provide intermediate activities or materials as a bridge. But regardless of the racial composition of the class, it is essential that the learning environment include not only materials with which a child is familiar but also a variety of cultural and ethnic materials with which she or he is not. Only in this way can children's own experiences and senses of culture be supported while they are being introduced to those of other ethnic groups.

Finally, the cultural appropriateness of curriculum materials, the content, and classroom practices are also instrumental in determining a child's predisposition to learning. For example, if discussions concerning death or divorce are not typical in a young child's family or ethnic group, a child may be reluctant to participate in a discussion of such matters in your class. To make the issues less charged, you might want to keep a variety of books about difficult times in families mixed in with the others in the book corner. You should also talk to the classroom parents to find out how (or if) they are talking about "sensitive" issues with their children and what their preferences are about dealing with tough issues in the classroom. The problem comes, of course, if some parents don't want any discussion in school of divorce or death. Patricia Ramsey (1987) writes about what to do when parents and teachers have different perspectives about what goes on in the classroom. One of her suggestions is that, as teacher, you step outside yourself to look at the cultural messages which have influenced the design of this aspect of the curriculum. Because it is important to do all that you can to see the parent's perspective clearly, mentally reverse roles with the parent, putting yourself in his or her place as much as possible. While there are no easy answers in a situation like this, the most important thing to remember is to enter into genuine dialogue with the parent. Regardless of where the conversation ends, it is essential that the parent feels treated respectfully and that you take the concerns of the parent seriously.

Sometimes children find it easier and more acceptable to deal with difficult concepts indirectly. It may be less threatening, for example, for some children to talk about the death of an animal than it is to talk about the death of a person. Often young children's questions about death and divorce are really questions about "What can I control?" The teacher can design a curriculum that will help children understand what things they can control and what things they cannot. For instance, we can control some of the ways we move our bodies, but not how tall we grow. We can control our behavior, but we often can't control our feelings. We aren't able to control whether or not someone dies or parents get divorced, and that is usually very hard for children to accept.

The manner in which an activity is carried out often affects how children respond. If children have learned at home that it is important to keep their clothes clean at school, they may have difficulty participating fully in painting a large and messy mural. Your providing smocks or play clothes for these children may allow them to participate more fully and freely in the project. By offering this option, you are doing two things. First, you are honoring the parents' needs and desires, and, second, you are avoiding a situation in which children could get caught between home and school. Teachers should be aware of their requests or directions and be prepared to offer children alternatives with which they will be more comfortable. In short, as a teacher, you play a critical role in influencing a child's predisposition to learn by providing children with an atmosphere that includes a variety of learning opportunities, by presenting information that is relevant to their environments and cultures, and by adapting the curriculum to make it appropriate to individual family concerns.

In addition to describing the three factors that influence a child's predisposition to learn, Longstreet (1978) describes six behavioral patterns that affect how learning takes place and that she feels might be influenced by culture:

1. The child's manner of participating in activities—whether she or he watches from the sidelines or gets enthusiastically involved
2. The attention she or he gives to activities—attending to one task at a time or doing several things at once
3. The ways in which she or he processes information—asking many questions as the teacher is talking or taking information in, thinking about it, and coming back later with questions
4. The manner in which the child presents her or his thoughts to others—teaching another child how to complete a task by telling her or him about it or by demonstrating the activity
5. The ways in which she or he asks questions—carefully, fearing that there might be a risk to admitting ignorance, or with abandon, believing that the way to discover something is to ask
6. The kinds of questions the child asks—intimate ones like "Why are you so skinny?" or careful and circumscribed ones, like "Do you think that flower is pretty?"

Again, by carefully observing children in a classroom you can find patterns that demonstrate how a child's learning style affects her or his participation in the group. Jotting down daily or weekly notes on what is observed can help you to discover patterns of interaction with peers and materials.

In order to accommodate the various learning styles of the children in a classroom, you have two responsibilities. First, you need to be aware of your own ways of learning, which have been determined by your own ethnicity, life experiences, and personality. You can find out about your learning style by examining the same behavioral patterns in yourself that you would in a child to identify hers or his. Through this awareness you will be better able to recognize your own tendencies toward ethnocentrism and will be more apt to fashion your approaches to teaching to fit the various ways the children learn. (See the Cultural Bias Checklist in Chapter 3, Figure 3.3, as one way for you to discover more about how you see the world.) Second, by providing a flexible classroom environment, you encourage all the children to learn. By being sensitive to children's learning and by being aware of the cultural influences on their styles, you offer each child the opportunity to grow and learn in ways most suitable to her or him. Further, in a classroom in which many learning styles are encouraged, more styles of problem solving and decision making are available for children to choose from.

THE DEVELOPMENT OF RACIAL AWARENESS AND RACIAL ATTITUDES

Children are frequently thought of as being "color-blind," that is, unaware of what color or race people are. However, this idea is contradicted by facts. Young children are very aware of race and color differences (Spencer & Markstrom-Adams, 1990). They ask frequent questions, most often related to their own physical characteristics and those of others, about matters such as skin color and hair color (Derman-Sparks, Higa, & Sparks, 1980).

There is general agreement among researchers that the development of children's racial awareness has begun by age 3 or 4. By that time children seem to recognize what color skin individuals have (Katz, 1976). Some theorists (for example, Goodman, 1952/1964) believe that this recognition is part of young children's process of establishing their identities; children recognize what they are and what they are not.

Positive and negative feelings about race seem to appear at about the same age as awareness of race. In Goodman's (1952/1964) classic study of 103 Black and White children, 25% of the White children exhibited some negative feelings about Black people; one child, for example, talked about wanting to cut a Black man's head off with an ax. In a study done in the North-

east with 3- to 5-year-old children (Porter, 1969), White children were more
positive about their skin colors than Black children were about theirs. The
White children applied positive adjectives to their colors; Black children
applied less positive adjectives to their skin colors. In a study done by Southern California day-care workers recording young children's comments about
race (Derman-Sparks et al., 1980), a frequently reported question from Black
children was "Why do I have to be Black?" An interesting addition to this
research was reported in Ann Beuf's 1977 study. She found that the Native
American children she interviewed were clear that being White was better,
not because being Native American was, in and of itself, not as good, but
because the White people they knew were richer and had more power. Already
these 5-year-olds understood that the White people were the teachers and that
non-White people could only be aides.

Although there is much evidence to show that the foundations of negative racial attitudes are laid sometime during the preschool years (Williams
& Morland, 1976), how these judgments are developed is a question debat-
ed by many researchers. Some have focused on parents' beliefs as determinants of children's attitudes. Morris (1981) reported, for example, that teachers in her study held parents responsible for their children's negative feelings
about race. Although there is no substantive data to support this hypothesis, this notion is still widely held.

Other researchers believe that children's negative racial beliefs are reinforced by the culture in general—by media, by adults, and by peers. Citron
(1971) states that children's attitudes are shaped by the segregated nature
of society; White children are under the illusion that they are the only children in the world, and children of color see themselves as different from
and less worthy than the rest. Stabler and Jordan (1971) and Porter (1969)
argue that children's negative racial attitudes are due in part to their internalization of the positive associations of the word *white* and the negative associations of the word *black* in the English language. Still another researcher
(P. A. Katz, 1976) believes that negative attitudes are caused by the combination of these factors rather than any single one. Twenty years after most
of this research was carried out we are still unable to say with certainty all that
is involved in the development of these attitudes.

This uncertainty concerning the precise causes of negative racial attitudes makes your job as a teacher all the more difficult. If it were established,
for example, that children learned their racial values only from their parents, then energy could be focused on working with parents. However, failure so far to isolate all of the elements responsible for developing racial attitudes does not imply that nothing can be done. For, as Morris (1981) states,
"Direct experiences, observations and internalization of concepts inherent
in the environment are powerful determinants of children's attitudes and

behaviors" (p. 236). Thus teachers who are trying to combat the development of negative racial judgments in children can work to create an environment in which children develop a sense both of themselves and of those from different cultural backgrounds as vital, worthwhile people, each with uniqueness and value.

This chapter has focused on three large issues: the development of children, the variety of learning styles, and the development of racial attitudes. One connecting theme is that, to varying degrees, each is affected by culture and ethnicity. Children grow and develop in the context of the cultural norms and values of their families. Their approaches to discovering new information are affected by cultural rules about what are and are not appropriate ways of exploring. Judgments about those who are "different" are deeply contextual. In many homes in the United States, people who eat beef are considered normal, while in India those people would be outcasts because there cattle are sacred. In Western European cultures, there are no real negative attitudes about people who sit cross-legged, showing the soles of their shoes to others; in Arab cultures, people who sit that way are considered unspeakably rude.

Another thread running through these issues is that, in each case, there is an enormous amount that is unknown. The fields of child development and early childhood education are reexamining the foundations of developmental theory in order to take into account the effects of culture and ethnicity on children and their preferred ways of learning. And, while a great deal of research has been done on the development of children's racial attitudes, we still don't know exactly how the judgments of the young child become the attitudes and biases of the adult. Surely that process, too, is related to the individual child's cultural context. There is much still to be studied in each of these areas, and our findings will clearly have impact on how multicultural education moves forward. Our task is to continue to probe and to be willing to deconstruct what we thought we knew in order to get to a deeper understanding.

Taking the Emotional Risk—
Examining Ourselves and
Our Attitudes

One morning while waiting for a trendy clothing outlet to open, I began to talk with a young White woman who was just finishing her student teaching at a nearby urban university. I asked where she planned to teach, and she replied that she would look for a job in a suburban school, that "teaching children in urban areas was too much of an emotional risk." My stomach tightened and my throat closed. My tact fell by the wayside. "If that's too much of a risk," I heard myself say, "why are you teaching at all?"

The purpose of this chapter is to provide a way for looking at ourselves as teachers working with children and families in the last half of the 1990s and moving into the new millennium. Teaching is getting harder and harder; being a genuinely good teacher requires an enormous amount of mental and physical energy and the willingness to look at things we're not so sure we want to know about. Still, central to my beliefs about education is that teachers who want to address effectively issues of multiculturalism must be willing to involve their minds and hearts in working with children and adults—that is, they must be willing to take emotional risks.

For me, "taking the emotional risk" requires:

- Understanding the societal context in which I am teaching
- Addressing the extraordinarily complex issues of racism, sexism, cul-

tural differences, sexual orientation, and class in myself and with my colleagues in an ongoing and intentional way
- Being open in mind and heart, willing to listen and to change
- Seeing myself, *always*, as a learner; working with children, parents, and other teachers and staff with an attitude of humility and cooperativeness

Let's look at how each of these traits applies to our development as teachers and how they lay the groundwork for genuine multicultural education. "Taking the emotional risk" involves examining our own attitudes, particularly those about race. This is a continuing, difficult process for all people because racial attitudes are deeply ingrained. It is important to keep in mind that the goal of exploring racial attitudes is not immediate basic change but, rather, awareness of attitudes and examination of behaviors. It is unrealistic to expect our deepest selves to change quickly, but behaviors can be altered right away. When the teacher in the university community child-care center was made aware that she washed her hands after touching African American children, the difficult and lengthy work of changing attitudes began. But, with careful attention, she could change her behavior at once.

UNDERSTANDING THE SOCIETAL CONTEXT

Exploring attitudes about race begins with some basic definitions. Although *prejudice, discrimination,* and *racism* are all part of the same problem, they are not the same, and each presents itself in different ways in our society.

Prejudice is defined as "an unfavorable feeling or opinion formed beforehand or without knowledge, thought, or reason" and as "unreasonable feelings, opinions, or attitudes, esp. of a hostile nature, regarding a racial, religious, or national group" (*Random House Dictionary,* 1993). A prejudice is an attitude: Johnny does not like Yolanda because she is Puerto Rican; Yolanda does not like Johnny because he is White. Ms. Jones does not like Ms. Greenberg because Ms. Greenberg is Jewish; Ms. Greenberg does not like Ms. Jones because Ms. Jones is a lesbian. There are a lot of unpleasant feelings, and, in fact, serious behavior, both violent and nonviolent, can stem from prejudice. Prejudice is an interpersonal matter between individuals or between an individual and a group of people.

Discrimination has its basis in prejudice, but, because it is behavior and not feeling, the consequences are more serious than those of prejudice. Ms. Lopez is not promoted from assistant principal to principal because she is a Latina; Ms. Boynton disciplines her pupil Jake more severely because he is Black and male. Mr. Takimoto is not elected to the school board because he is Japanese American. Each of these people is discriminated against on the basis of her or his color. They are not treated as they would have been had they been White. People of color can also discriminate against White people. A working definition of *discrimination* is "treatment...of...a person or thing based on the group, class, or category to which that person or thing belongs rather than on individual merit" (*Random House Dictionary,* 1993).

The implications of racism are more far-reaching than those of either prejudice or discrimination. *Racism* is defined as "any attitude, action, or institutional structure which subordinates a person or group because of his or their color" (U.S. Commission on Civil Rights, 1970). The key to this definition is subordination. Individuals or groups of people are kept in subordinate, less powerful, less important positions on the basis of color. *Random House Dictionary* (1993) defines *racism* as "a belief or doctrine that inherent differences among the various human races determine cultural or individual achievement, usually involving the idea that one's own race is superior and has the right to rule others" and "a policy, system of government, etc., based upon or fostering such a doctrine."

One aspect of racism is *cultural racism.* Cultural racism is racism that is so much a part of the mainstream culture that it looks "normal." It outlives any single individual and pervades the thinking, speech, and actions of whole groups of people. In the English language, for example, many of our positive definitions and connotations of the word *white* and negative connotations of the word *black* reinforce notions of White superiority and Black inferiority (Burgest, 1973). "White lies" are not as bad as others; we "whitewash" something to gloss over the problem; white is seen as the color of purity and so, in European American cultures, brides wear white dresses and have white wedding cakes. On the other hand, black cats are dangerous; we talk about bad days as "black" days; in movies, good guys wear white hats and bad guys wear black hats. Until very recently, a flesh-colored crayon corresponded more closely to the color of White people's skin than that of any other. As of this writing, that is still the case with Band-Aids. *Cultural racism* is revealed in the casual racial stereotyping in expressions like "sitting Indian style" or counting Native Americans as if they were objects when we sing "One little, two little, three little Indians." (Do we sing "One little, two little, three little White people"?) Expressions like "Chinese fire drill," "Mexican stand-off," or "Jew him down" reinforce and help create the biases reflected in everyday English; they also demonstrate deeply ingrained cultural racism.

Institutional structures (schools and school boards, courts, police departments, legal and medical institutions, social-service departments, and so on) that subordinate a person or group because of color are part of the most pernicious and pervasive form of racism. *Institutional racism* is so embedded in our society's structures that those of us who are part of the "mainstream" or "regular" (read "White") group don't see ourselves as personally responsible for, or often even personally connected to, its perpetuation. (For further discussion of this, see the definition of *privilege* later in this section.) An example of institutional racism in the area of education is the continued use of culturally biased IQ tests, such as the Wechsler Intelligence Scale for Children–Revised (WISC-R), that "elevate the mean score for Anglo children...and...define groups that differ systematically in their language, values, or behavioral style from the majority group as abnormal" (Mercer, 1979, p. 20). As Cole and Cole (1993) tell us,

> all tests of intelligence draw on a background of learning that is culture-specific....[This] greatly limits the conclusions that can be drawn from IQ testing in different social and cultural groups. (p. 502)

An example helps us understand this problem. On an achievement test, children are given four letters—"A," "C," "T," and "O"—and asked to make a word from them. The children who make *COAT* are given two points; the children who make *TACO* are not. This is what is meant by "culturally biased" tests; the children for whom Spanish is their first language might be more likely to make *TACO* than the children whose dominant language is English and whose culture is Western European.

In our educational system, as in every other institution in contemporary society, *institutional racism* is prevalent. Brief looks at the areas of curriculum, ability grouping, and the lack of diverse role models illustrate some of the ways in which institutional racism manifests itself. Curriculum materials are, perhaps, the most obvious of all examples. (Remember the alphabet charts that have "I is for Indian" or "Igloo" or "E is for Eskimo"?) Although some improvements have been made in this area, materials still contain stereotyped representations of people of non-White races. Even today, after years of protest against stereotypes in educational materials, books, tapes, pictures, and other audiovisuals continue to inform children that Indians live in teepees, that Black people make loud music, and that Chinese people operate laundries.

Another example of institutional racism in schools is seen in curriculum priorities. Because a curriculum reflects the values and priorities of those who devise it (Chesler, 1967), it is important to look at what is put into the curriculum and what is omitted. For example, in an attempt to address the issue of cultural awareness, some designers of curricula include a month to study African Americans, a week to study Native Americans, and a month to study Hispanics/Latinos, without integrating a multicultural approach into the rest of the year's program. Although celebrating African American History Month is an improvement on the old ways, eleven "White months" remain in the calendar year during which children continue to be taught in an ethnocentric manner. There are attempts being made in texts and in books to reflect a more realistic and inclusive picture of United States history, but we still have a long way to go.

Ability grouping, or the tracking system, is another way in which children of color suffer discrimination and institutional racism is maintained. The groups in which children are placed are often determined by the children's scores on IQ and achievement tests which we have already seen are culturally biased to reward White middle-class children and penalize others. When children are tracked, White middle-class children who are placed in gifted and talented programs frequently come to feel that all children in the lower tracks are inferior, particularly those of color. Children in the slower groups feel bad about themselves because of their positions in the tracking system. Children of color in the higher groups think that being a person of color is not as good as being White or there would be more children like them in their groups. Finally, children often remain in the ability groups they are placed in at the beginning of their schooling, and frequently they achieve only to that level of expectation, regardless of their intelligence (Holt, 1982). (For further discussion of self-fulfilling prophecy and teacher expectations, see Gilligan, 1990; Rosenthal, 1987; Rosenthal & Jacobsen, 1968; and Sadker & Sadker, 1994, among others.)

A lack of role models for children of color reinforces the messages given by the tracking system. Despite an increased number of African Americans, Native Americans, Asian Americans, and Latinos in positions of authority, there is still a notable imbalance of power in the schools. The great majority of principals and assistant principals in our educational institutions are male. According to the 1992 census (U.S. Department of Commerce, 1994), 60% of school administrators are men. While this percentage is down from 79% in 1982, the number is still disproportionate to the number of men and women in education. In 1992, 80% of principals were White, as opposed to 84% in 1982. This does *not* mean that they are not doing good jobs. As in all situations, there is a range; some are doing great jobs and some are mediocre. What it does mean is that all children, regardless of race or gender, see White men in charge. Even if this message is not spoken aloud, it is presented nonverbally. In the absence of alternative authority figures, children can assume that White men are the only people who can run things. Further, White girls and boys and girls of color might not strive for decision-making jobs because of their lack of role models. At the same time that children see White men in positions of authority in schools, they frequently see adults of color in more menial jobs, serving as teacher's aides, janitors, and cooks in the cafeterias. This institutionalized racial imbalance reinforces children's perceptions that some people are destined to hold leadership positions while others are inherently unable to do so. Further, the relative absence of White women and people of color in positions of authority leads children to believe that ability is race- and gender-based.

Sexism, homophobia and *heterosexism, anti-bias, antiracism,* and *privilege* are a few of the other words we encounter in the context of discussing multicultural education. *Sexism* is defined as "attitudes or behavior based on traditional stereotypes of sexual roles" and "discrimination or devaluation based on a person's sex, as in restricted job opportunities; esp. such discrimination directed against women" (*Random House Dictionary,* 1993). Like racism, sexism is personal and institutional and is deeply rooted in all cultures.

Homophobia and *heterosexism* both refer to the issues facing gay men, lesbians, and bisexuals. *Homophobia* is the "unreasoning fear of or antipathy toward homosexuals and homosexuality" (*Random House Dictionary,* 1993) and is basically the personal hatred of those who are not heterosexual, a prejudice. *Heterosexism* is parallel to racism and sexism in that it is institutionalized "attitude[s] or discriminatory practices against homosexuals by heterosexuals" (*Random House Dictionary,* 1993). Heterosexism is the subordination of one group by another on the basis of sexual orientation.

Anti-bias is a term that became more familiar in 1989 when Louise Derman-Sparks published the *Anti-Bias Curriculum,* designed by her and her colleagues at Pacific Oaks College to provide "tools for empowering young children." Like *Diversity in the Classroom,* the *Anti-Bias Curriculum* is based on the notion that antiracism work is integral to good education for all children. *Anti-bias,* as Derman-Sparks defines it, is

> an active/activist approach to challenging prejudice, stereotyping, bias, and the "isms." In a society in which institutional structures create and maintain sexism, racism, and handicappism, it is not sufficient to be non-biased...nor is it sufficient to be an observer. It is necessary for each individual to actively intervene, to challenge and counter the personal and institutional behaviors that perpetuate oppression. (p. 3)

Antiracism is similar to *anti-bias,* although pertaining solely to intentional behaviors aimed at eliminating personal and institutional racism, as opposed to the broader *anti-bias* which addresses many "isms." As Sonia Nieto (1992) tells us, "Antiracism, and anti-discrimination in general, is at the very core of a multicultural perspective" (p. 208). She goes on to say, "To be antiracist also means to work affirmatively to combat racism. It means making antiracism and anti-discrimination an explicit part of the curriculum and teaching young people skills in confronting racism" (p. 210).

Privilege, particularly White or male privilege, is hard to see for those of us who were born with access to power and resources. It is very visible for those to whom privilege was not granted. Furthermore, the subject is extremely difficult to talk about because many White people don't feel powerful or as if they have privileges that others do not. It is sort of like asking fish to notice water or birds to discuss air. For those who have privileges based on race or gender or class or physical ability or sexual orientation or age, it just is—it's normal. *Random House Dictionary* (1993) defines *privilege* as "a right, immunity, or benefit enjoyed only by a person beyond the advantages of most." As Peggy McIntosh (1995) tells us, we usually believe that privileges are "conditions of daily experience...[that are] universally available to everybody." She goes on to say that what we are really talking about is "unearned power conferred systemically" (pp. 82–83).

McIntosh lists 54 examples of White privilege—"unearned power conferred systemically." Here are ten of them:

- I can go shopping alone most of the time, fairly well assured that I will not be followed or harassed by store detectives....
- I can turn on the television or open to the front page of the paper and see people of my race widely and positively represented....
- When I am told about our national heritage or about "civilization," I am shown that people of my color made it what it is....
- I can be sure that my children will be given curricular materials that testify to the existence of their race....
- I can be pretty sure that my children's teachers and employers will tolerate them if they fit school and workplace norms; my chief worries about them do not concern others' attitudes toward their race....
- I can swear, or dress in secondhand clothes, or not answer letters without having people attribute these choices to the bad morals, the poverty, or the illiteracy of my race....
- I am never asked to speak for all of the people of my racial group....
- I can remain oblivious to the language and customs of persons of color who constitute the world's majority without feeling in my culture any penalty for such oblivion....
- I can easily buy posters, postcards, picture books, greeting cards, dolls, toys, and children's magazines featuring people of my race....
- I am not made acutely aware that my shape, bearing, or body odor will be taken as a reflection on my race....(pp. 79–80)

Lisa Delpit (1988) approaches the notion of privilege from a connected, but slightly different, angle. She has identified five premises concerning what she calls "the culture of power":

1. Issues of power are enacted in classrooms.
2. There are codes or rules for participating in power; that is, there is a "culture of power."
3. The rules of the culture of power are a reflection of the rules of those who have the power.

4. If you are not already a participant in the culture of power, being told explicitly the rules of that culture makes acquiring power easier.
5. Those with power are frequently least aware of—or least willing to acknowledge—its existence. Those with less power are often most aware of its existence. (p. 282)

Premises 1, 2, 3, and 5 have been addressed in various ways in this chapter and in Chapter 1, so I will discuss those only briefly. While we may be uncomfortable with the idea that power is enacted in our classrooms, there are lots of ways that power presents itself. Teachers have power over children as they discipline them, praise them, pay attention to them or don't; there is often a power dynamic between teachers and parents; there is power in determining what is taught and what is not. As with any culture, there are rules (of behavior, of inclusion and exclusion, of ways of speaking and language used), and those rules generally reflect the culture of the people in power. This is what Lillian Smith (1978) was talking about in her essay "The Winner Names the Age" (see Chapter 1). Reading the examples from McIntosh (1995), it is clear that those who have access to power and privilege are often not aware that they are powerful in ways that others are not; people who are excluded from "the culture of power" are much more conscious of the power dynamics.

Premise 4, "If you are not already a participant in the culture of power, being told explicitly the rules of that culture makes acquiring power easier," is very important in understanding how to create a genuinely equitable and hospitable educational environment for all. Essentially, Delpit is reminding us that all cultures, whether they are racial or organizational, have formal and informal rules. The formal rules are usually fairly accessible. For example, each school or classroom has an organizational culture and a set of explicit rules: child-care payments are due on the first of the month, no guns are allowed in school, if parents are late to pick up their children they will have to pay a fine of $10. Those rules are written down in a parent booklet given to each new family as it enters the school. Each culture also has a set of informal rules about everything from what is considered appropriate dress to how communication takes place. Those who have power in the culture know the rules and "transmit information [about them] implicitly to co-members" (p. 283). People who are part of the power-holding group at a school will know, for example, that the due date for payments is very important to the director and that, while other rules are not so important to her or him, this one is. Moreover, when parents, particularly poor White parents or parents of color, are late in their payments, they are labeled as freeloaders and put on the unwritten troublemakers' list. Parents who aren't part of the group with power, and haven't explicitly been told that in this case the informal rule matches the formal rule, will have no idea of the consequences of their actions.

Let's look at another example. In the day-care center in which I taught it was never explicitly stated, but it was expected that children would come to school dressed in play clothes. In addition, part of the school culture's informal rules was that it was not a big deal if a child got dirty. The middle-class White families had been told by their neighbors how to dress their children and so brought them to school in overalls. One of the more traditional Puerto Rican families, however, had a different cultural rule about the appropriate way to dress a little girl for school. The child arrived daily in an organdy dress and patent-leather shoes and with a bow in her hair. Rather than talking with the family about the school's informal rules for dress as I should have, I talked with other staff about why the family dressed her in a manner that seemed so inappropriate to *me*, one of the members of the culture of power. Finally I realized that I had not done my part in helping them understand what the informal expectations were so that the family could decide which of the cultural rules they wanted to follow. Had I mentioned those rules initially, the family could have chosen whether they wanted to fit into the school culture or abide by their own traditions. If they chose to continue to bring the child to school in frilly dresses, then it was my job to see that her clothes were protected when we painted or played outside.

A final example also points out the unconscious assumptions made by a teacher who was a member of the culture of power. Wanting the children in her class to do well in first grade, a kindergarten teacher began in September to provide opportunities for the students to learn to read. She created a rich language-arts environment in the classroom with lots of books and related materials. At the fall parent meeting, she explained her curriculum and asked the parents to reinforce what their children were learning at school by taking them to the public library at least once a month, buying books from the school book club, and reading stories aloud at home three or four times a week. For the parents of the middle-class children, the teacher's requests fit in with their own cultural and educational expectations. Reading was an important part of their families' leisure-time activities. These children thrived and, in fact, most of them were reading by January. Some of the non-White, non-mainstream children, however, were not faring so well. They were not terribly enthusiastic about reading and did it only if forced. The teacher, who had grown up in a house surrounded by books, had no idea that many families don't own books and either see no need to or can't afford to. Further, it never occurred to her that some of these parents were skimping on their own lunches in order to be able to buy books for their children from the school book club. Had the teacher been aware of the need to create equitable access to the culture of power, she would have talked explicitly from the beginning about her emphasis on reading. She would have broadened her approach to teaching reading in her classroom so that, while providing lots of language-arts experiences, she would also have taught concrete reading skills to the children. Finally, she would have been creative in finding financing for the book club so that parents would not have to deprive themselves or embarrass themselves and their children by saying they did not have money to buy books.

Teachers who understand the culture of power and its connection to institutional racism (sexism, heterosexism, and so on) in the educational system will be better able to create a genuinely inclusive and multicultural classroom environment. They will also have a better foundation from which to examine their own attitudes. And that leads us to the second aspect of taking the emotional risk.

EXPLORING OUR OWN ATTITUDES

One way to begin this process of addressing thorny issues in an ongoing and intentional way is to look at our own experiences with issues of race, to note our responses when the experiences occurred, and to look at our own present-day responses to such experiences. As a beginning, J. H. Katz (1978) suggests examining the following types of experiences:

1. The experience of first meeting a person of a different color, of realizing the similarities and differences in life experiences
2. The experience of discovering that school texts often misrepresent history or tell only part of the story (for example, realizing that slaves were not content on plantations in the South or discovering that thousands of Japanese Americans were interned in this country during World War II, though the majority of German Americans were not)
3. The experience of realizing that people are treated differently according to their color
4. The experience of being the only person of color in an all White group or the only White person among people of color

It would also be good to look at these four experiences as they pertain to someone who is from a culture other than yours rather than from another race. How are your responses similar or different?

Some of these experiences involving race are more directly related to teaching than others—for example, being an African American teacher with a class composed almost entirely of White children, or being a White, English-speaking teacher with a class of Hispanic children who speak Spanish at home. There are underlying commonalities among the school-related experiences mentioned above. Two factors are the sense of being different from the children and parents you work with and of having a separate set of racial experiences that you bring to the classroom. In such instances, it is helpful to look at the racial attitudes you hold about the group with which you're working and at how you feel about being the only person in a group who does not share a common cultural heritage.

It is also important to explore why you put yourself in the position of being "the other." Obviously there are some instances in which a teacher is assigned to a school without regard for her or his preference. In other situations, however, teachers choose to work with classes composed entirely of children from a different racial group than their own (or from a different socioeconomic class, for that matter). In the case of the White teacher of the Spanish-speaking class, is the motivation for such a choice wanting to "help" a group perceived to be "disadvantaged"? One of the clues that this is happening is when children are spoken of as "these children," as in "What these children need is..." or "These people should be happy with all that we are giving them." In the case of the African American teacher of an all-White class, is the motivation to prove that one's own racial group is competent and not so different from White people? What about a person who grew up in a wealthy family working in a school in a very poor community? Or a working-class person teaching at an exclusive private school? What are the implications and possible considerations in those situations? Clearly there are many things that would motivate a teacher to make such a choice—some emotional, some professional, and others financial. It is important, in terms of your own awareness of the attitudes with which you approach a job, to spend time identifying personal reasons for teaching in a class of children racially or culturally different from yourself.

The exercise in Figure 3.1 offers another avenue to exploring our attitudes about race, gender, sexual orientation, and physical ability. It is designed to help us understand that who we are as individuals, in terms of these categories, greatly affects how we see the world and how the world sees us. You can modify the exercise to include other aspects of difference, but don't take out categories that you think don't apply to you. For example, even if you don't have any male staff members, think about what a man's experience might be in your classroom. How welcome would lesbian or gay parents be at your school? How easy would it be for a deaf teacher to fit into your staff? How would you alter your school environment if you had families who had just recently arrived in the United States from Laos or Cambodia or Afghanistan or Russia or Chile?

This exercise is best used in a discussion group with others on your staff. To begin, work alone and fill out all parts of the exercise even though some of them don't specifically apply to you. For example, if you are biracial, describe what it means to be a biracial staff member, and then hypothesize what it would be like to be a member of the staff who was from only one

Figure 3.1 *To Me, Being...*

Please respond to *all* of the following questions as openly and thoughtfully as you can in preparation for talking with one another. (Obviously some of the questions apply directly to you and others will have to be answered somewhat hypothetically.)

1. To me, being a White staff member at _____ (your school's name) means...
2. To me, being a biracial/multiracial staff member at _____ means...
3. To me, being a staff member of color at _____ means...
4. To me, being a heterosexual staff member at _____ means...
5. To me, being a gay or lesbian staff member at _____ means...
6. To me, being a female staff member at _____ means...
7. To me, being a male staff member at _____ means...
8. To me, being a biracial/multiracial family at _____ means...
9. To me, being a White family at _____ means...
10. To me, being a family of color at _____ means...
11. To me, being a gay or lesbian family at _____ means...
12. To me, being a heterosexual family at _____ means...
13. How do *your ethnicity* and *culture* play roles in your responses?
14. What implications or ramifications might other differences have in the _____ community?
    Gender?
    Socioeconomic class?
    Physical ability?
    Age?
    Culture?
    Religion?
15. What other thoughts or feelings come up as you are responding to these questions?

© Frances E. Kendall, Ph.D.

racial group. After responding to all of the questions, move into small groups (3–5 people) for approximately 30 minutes and go through the statements one by one, talking about how each of you felt as you wrote your answers. Then form a large group and talk about your small group conversations. There are two key lessons to be learned in this exercise. First, it gives us an opportunity to step into other people's shoes, if only for a minute, to see how their experiences might differ from our own. Second, completing the exercise enables us to pinpoint where we, as a staff, have work to do to make our school or class more hospitable to all people.

So far I have focused predominantly on examining our racial attitudes because our literal survival as a nation rests on our ability to face what Studs Terkel has called "the American obsession" (1992). However, it is not wise to ignore other aspects of difference as we look at our attitudes and behaviors. It is my experience and conviction that, until we have done our work on all issues of difference, we haven't really done our work on any of them. Far too frequently people say to me, "I'm not prejudiced. I have Black friends, Jewish friends, friends who are disabled. I don't really have any prejudices." And, at the same time, that person won't hire an openly gay teacher because, "Well, I don't know. I just don't think it would be a good idea. I'm not prejudiced, but homosexuality is another matter." Or people say, "I'm all for having a culturally diverse population in our school, as long as 'they' do things the way we do them." I also hear, "It's not that I don't like men; I just don't want them in our center." And recently, a parent commented on a new teacher from a working-class background, "I like her a lot, but she doesn't speak good English. I don't think she will be a good model for the children."

The issues of sexual orientation, socioeconomic class, and cultural differences are, at this point in our nation's history, three of the most confounding. In some ways our approaches to them should be similar to our approach to race: learn as much as you can; look deeply and honestly at the areas with which you are uncomfortable; involve yourself in conversations with people who feel differently as well as similarly to you and people who are different from you as well as similar. Push yourself to grapple with the most perplexing questions. As my friend and colleague David Tulin says, "Become more comfortable with the uncomfortable and less comfortable with the too comfortable." If you are a member of the culture of power, one of the most difficult yet potentially rewarding conversations is with another White (or male or heterosexual) person. Through these interactions it is possible to interrupt hurtful behavior and create a ripple effect of change throughout the empowered group. A conversation between two White people might begin like this (the same exchanges as might occur about gender or sexual orientation):

> "I'm so tired of hearing those people [African Americans] talk about racism. That's all they ever talk about."
> "Well, maybe they would talk less about it if *we* talked more about it. It is our problem, you know. Let's have lunch with Karl and see what's on his mind and what we can do. It might not be an easy lunch, but maybe if somebody listened to him for once he wouldn't have to keep repeating himself."

There are ways in which sexual orientation, class, and cultural differences need to be addressed differently. For example, in my experience, we are more likely to be clear and vocal about our biases about and discomfort with gay men and lesbians than we are about people who are culturally different. It is impossible to overstate the impact of negative comments on all children and their families, particularly when they are made by teachers. Children who discover as they grow older that they are gay have already received years of negative information about who they are. The U.S. Department of Health and Human Services believes that these messages contribute heavily to gay and bisexual suicides. They estimate that lesbian, gay, and bisexual youths are two to three times more likely to try to kill themselves than heterosexual youths, and that they account for 30% of all completed suicides (Gibson, 1989). Children who grow up to be heterosexual have also heard many negative comments about gay, lesbian, and bisexual people, some of whom might be family members or close friends. They become confused about how to relate to someone they love but about whom they have heard terrible things. It is the early childhood educator's responsibility to address her or his prejudices about bisexuals, gay men, and lesbians. While it might not be a group that you would choose to belong to or you may have religious beliefs that keep you from valuing gay people, it is essential that you learn to manage your biases.

It is difficult to talk about socioeconomic class because the myth is that the United States is a classless society, yet our class biases were inculcated so early in our development that we had no idea how much direction we were getting. I visited a very socioeconomically and racially diverse preschool recently. It was a Monday morning following winter break and the teacher gathered the children together for circle time. She began a conversation by asking the children what they had done during their vacation. The first child talked about going skiing at Lake Tahoe; the second described a visit to her grandmother's in Vermont. I watched as the poorer children sloughed over their vacation experiences, frequently saying, "Oh, I didn't really do anything." A teacher who is aware of the range of socioeconomic levels among the children won't set up situations in which the differences are so obvious. Rather than asking what they did for vacation, she might ask the children to mention people they saw or games they played or meals they ate.

Another challenge is that we have to be aware of our *own* expectations of the roles differences play before we can begin to look at other people with any kind of objectivity and understanding. For example, heterosexual teachers who have had little experience with gay people tend to expect that heterosexual parents will have radically different values and beliefs from gay and lesbian parents. In fact, for most of the individual lesbians, gay men, or bisexuals that a heterosexual meets, sexual orientation is the main way that he or she differs. In other variables—class, racial heritage, national heritage, education, and values—the two people are apt to be similar. While we expect to be very different, we often are not, and our similarities surprise us. On the other hand, when meeting people who are culturally different from us, our sexual orientations are more likely to be the same (at least for heterosexuals), but in many other basic ways—how we live, what we value, what our belief systems are—we are apt to be very different. And we are often surprised by those differences: "I thought if I just followed the Golden Rule and treated everyone the same we would all get along." It doesn't work that way because the Golden Rule is class- and culture-specific. How we want to be treated is more likely to be determined by what we have each learned based on socioeconomic class and culture than what is based solely on sexual orientation.

Bearing all this in mind, two exercises are included as Figure 3.2 and Figure 3.3 to aid in identifying the ethnic and cultural messages we have received. First, let's be clear about what we mean by *ethnicity* and *culture*. To review the definition in Chapter 2, *culture* is a people's way of doing things, a system of rules for making meaning of the universe, a system of values and beliefs that affect our behavior. Culture is learned. *Ethnicity* has to do with one's ethnic group and national origin. We are born with our ethnicity. Within each race of people there are many ethnic groups: Irish, Mandarin, Polish, Japanese, Masai, Cherokee, Haitian, and so on. In Native American culture, tribes are very much like ethnic groups, each with its own distinct culture and geographic origin.

Fill out Exploring Your Own Ethnicity and Culture (Figure 3.2) on your own or with other people with whom you work. This exercise can be used for a variety of purposes: to begin to look at some of the early messages you were given; to better understand how what you were taught creeps into your own behavior with children, either consciously or unconsciously; to open con-

---

Figure 3.2 *Exploring Your Own Ethnicity and Culture*

DIRECTIONS: Answer each of the following questions in relation to you and the family in which you grew up.

1. How did your family think children *should* be raised?
2. What were their hopes for you? What were their expectations for you? How important were school and education?
3. What were the roles and responsibilities of mother, father, and children? If you lived with only one parent, on what basis were tasks divided?
4. What were your family's religious beliefs and practices?
5. How were you disciplined? What were your family's attitudes about discipline?
6. What were your family's attitudes about sex?
7. What messages did you receive about cultural differences and how were they presented? From whom did you get the messages?

---

versations with people you work with. There is no right or wrong answer to any of the questions. It is important, though, to make connections between what you were taught about gender roles of mothers and fathers, for example, and how you view the parents in your class or the behaviors of boys and girls in your center. As with the other exercises included in this book, spend time in small and large groups discussing your responses to the questions and how your own experiences might have impact on your work with the parents and children in your class and the staff members with whom you work.

The purpose of the Cultural Bias Checklist (Figure 3.3) is to look at some of the subtle cultural biases we hold. Because they are held, to a great extent, unconsciously, we frequently act on the basis of those perspectives without having any idea that that is what we are doing. We assume that everybody defines each of the words in the exercise as we would define it and that everyone feels as we feel about the words. Moreover, we often attribute these biases (if we see them as biases at all) to our individual personalities, rather than seeing them as products of our cultural heritage. In fact, each of these words is value-laden, and the meaning or value placed on the word is culturally constructed. For example, *distant* means very different things in various cultures. If we are not clear about how *distant* looks from our cultural perspective and cannot describe the quality, we won't be able to communicate with others who might define it differently.

Let's look at another example. One of the choices on the Cultural Bias Checklist is *team player*. I once spent a day with a staff of maintenance people, all men, who were absolutely unable to work with one another. Roughly half of the men were Latino and half were African American. When asked to identify the problems they were having with each other, both groups said that the others were not good "team players." I asked each group to describe what being a good team player was. The members of one group said, "For us, being a team player means doing your own job the very best you can so that no one else will have to take responsibility for your part." The other group had an entirely different, and, in fact, contradictory, sense of what the words meant. "We believe that being a good team player means dropping whatever you are doing to go and help someone else. We each see the whole job as our responsibility so it is not terribly important which person does what part." Until the men came to a *shared* understanding of what being a good team member meant for them as a whole group, their conflict was not going to be resolved. Both groups had erroneously assumed that everyone defined *team player* as they had learned to early in life and that "the others" were simply lazy and shirking their responsibilities.

When I use the Cultural Bias Checklist with groups, *false* is frequently chosen as a quality not liked. Like most of the other words, the definition of *false* is culturally constructed. Some define it as *lying*, others as *two-faced*, oth-

Figure 3.3 *Cultural Bias Checklist*

Circle five adjectives describing people you like, and underline five adjectives describing people you do not like to be around. You may add adjectives of your own.

adventurous	forgiving	self-satisfied
affectionate	fun-loving	sentimental
ambitious	gives praise readily	shows love
anxious for approval	good listener	shrewd, devious
appreciative	helpful	shy
argumentative	indifferent to others	sociable
big-hearted	impulsive	stern
candid	independent	submissive
competitive	intolerant	successful
complaining	jealous	sympathetic
critical of others	kind	tactful
demanding	loud	talkative
discourteous	neat	team player
distant	needs much praise	teasing
dogmatic	obedient	thorough
dominating	optimistic	thoughtful
easily angered	orderly	touchy, cannot be kidded
easily discouraged	rebellious	uncommunicative
easily influenced	resentful	understanding
efficient	responsible	varied interests
encouraging	sarcastic	very dependent on others
enthusiastic	self-centered	warm
false	self-respecting	well-mannered
		willing worker

DISCUSSION:

For each of the words you have chosen, think about what the word means to *you*. Where did this value originate for you? How might each of the descriptions you have selected be related to your *cultural* perspective? How might each affect your work style? What strategies might you use in working with someone who has one of the five qualities you like? What strategies might you use in working with someone who has one of the five qualities you don't like?

ers as *tricky*. A Latina director described this scenario: "I work with a Chinese teacher. When she came to our center I explained how we prepared our lesson plans and asked if she understood. She said she did. But when she turned hers in to me, they were totally wrong. Why did she lie? Why didn't she just tell me she didn't understand?"

Chances are good that the Chinese woman did not see herself as lying or as being "false." "Saving face" is valued very highly in Asian cultures. It is important not to embarrass yourself by appearing stupid—and not to embarrass someone else by insinuating that she or he did a poor job explaining. So, for some Asian people, the issue is about "saving face," not about telling a lie. The director who was working with the Chinese teacher had several ways, other than asking, to determine if the woman knew how to do lesson plans the way the director wanted them done. She could show how she herself did them and then ask the teacher to create one in the same manner; they could do one or two together; the director could give the new teacher a partner to work with for the first couple of months. Actually, there are many cultures that value other things more highly than by-the-letter truthfulness. In American Southern culture, for example, it is seen as ungracious to refuse food. So, even if you have just finished an enormous meal before arriving at someone's house, it would be considered impolite not to accept at least a little of what the person was offering you. In other American cultures, when someone asks you how you are that day, the appropriate answer is "Fine, thank you, and you?" even though you might have had a fight with your dog and feel a terrible cold coming on. If we remember that most of how we see the world is affected by the cultural messages we received as young children, we are more likely to be open to the cultural messages others operate from and be able to create a shared communication together.

Like the exercise on ethnicity and culture, the Cultural Bias Checklist can be done alone or with a group. The most valuable learning, however, comes from conversation with others who are culturally different from you. It is important to identify where your biases came from and how they guide the ways you work with other adults and children.

BEING WILLING TO LISTEN AND CHANGE

During our teacher training, many of us developed a very clear picture of what "good" practices are for working with young children. We based that picture on a system of values and beliefs, our knowledge of child development, and our sense of the best environment in which children can grow. Now we are having to reexamine much of what we saw as "good" in our work with families, staff, and children. The current population in nursery schools, preschools, and child-care centers looks very different from the one on which our long-held beliefs were based. And the population will grow increasingly varied in the coming years. Thus we come to the third aspect of taking emotional risk. For those of us who work with children, one of our greatest assets will be the ability and willingness to listen to people who bring very different ideas,

experiences, and needs to the educational setting. An open heart and an open mind are no longer luxuries; they have become necessities.

In some ways it feels as if everything is on the table; we need to relook, reconceptualize, reexamine, rethink. As Alice Walker says in "Reassurance" (1973), those of us who long for answers "...must love the questions" (p. 33). Our goal is to foster development that will have as its outcome healthy children as seen from *their* community's perspective. However, I must acknowledge some of my own limits on encouraging everything that other cultures allow. I struggled as I watched a 4-year-old boy from a Middle Eastern culture berating and hitting his mother at a child-care center in which I was working. I knew that he had been taught that such behavior is acceptable. In his culture women are very much second-class citizens—a male, regardless of age, is more valued than a female. Had the child been White and middle class, I would have felt more freedom—appropriately or not—to step in and stop the child. In this instance I was much slower to act. I did tell the mother that I was very uncomfortable with her son's treatment of her. I also said to her that at our school he wouldn't be allowed to hit anyone, not children or teachers. I don't know if I did the "right" thing. My challenge, as I saw it, was to be honest about my own feelings while not criticizing the family or their culture. None of this is easy; all of it requires being open in heart and willing to listen.

Another challenge is to prepare children who are not White and middle class—children of color, poor White children, immigrants, and so on—to know enough about how mainstream American culture works to be able to fit in to the extent that they ultimately want to. Obviously, young children won't be able to make that decision, so our job is to give them information that makes sense to them. Let's go back to the situation of the young Middle Eastern boy who was berating and hitting his mother. In addition to letting him know that he can't hit others at school, I can also tell him that in the United States most people don't think it is okay for a child to hit his mother. I might go on to say that, even though it appears to be acceptable in his home, other children and parents could shy away from him. In a sense, we are working to develop children who are bicultural—able to thrive in their own culture and in the dominant culture as well.

This is not, of course, the first time the need to be bicultural has occurred. Parents of color, particularly Blacks and Latinos, have for many years prepared their children to live in two worlds. African Americans talk about having to leave their "Black selves" at home when they come to work in business and academic settings. For more about this, see Bell, 1992; Cose, 1993; and Williams, 1991, listed and annotated in Appendix A. Carol Gilligan's (1990) research on adolescent girls at Emma Willard tells us that girls and women in Western culture have to learn to think in ways that differ from ways they are accustomed to thinking in order to fit into a system designed for and run by men. That is another kind of biculturalism.

What we are talking about in the last of the 20th century and the beginning of the 21st is creating schools and curricula that seriously consider children's culture, their home-based languages, and the expectations of their families. All children deserve our best efforts at finding out about them and their cultures and fashioning an environment in which they are comfortable enough to rise to the challenges of growing and learning. We are also responsible for helping children acquire skills that the mainstream thinks are important so that they will not miss opportunities to become who they want to be in the world. At the same time, there is a great deal of tension in the field of early childhood education (not to mention the in country as a whole) about how to create education that is really multicultural, whether we should, what happens if we do, what happens if we don't, and if teachers have the skills to teach in such a manner. In some parts of the country, the question is no longer whether we should but *how*. For example, more than half of the school children in California speak English as a second language. Many of the school districts there now require that teachers demonstrate competence in "crosscultural language and academic development" for children whose first language is not English. It is clear that a teacher is not fully prepared to teach in California—or in any other state—without skills in working with children from a variety of cultures.

There are many fears about what it means to develop an educational process that is truly inclusive of all who are part of this country. Much of the tension comes from teachers who feel inadequate to meet the changing needs of their school populations. Teachers fear they won't know what to do when the child's culture and the school's culture come into conflict. Often, when we talk about creating a school environment in which each child's culture is supported, our fears rise. We then move to our worst nightmares and choose examples of cultural behaviors that we believe will do damage to the child: "Does this *really* mean that we are going to have to support an African girl-child's having her clitoris removed in a clitoridectomy?" I heard myself asking a colleague. Obviously, it is an extreme example, but one that reflects my fear that we will have to give up many values we cherish. I believe that this is often a red herring thrown up because we are afraid of change. Many people of Western European descent have been led by politicians to fear a loss of America as they know it. The same fears were voiced when the Irish came to this country in large numbers in the mid-1800s and again when Italians came in the early 1900s (Lieberson, 1980). Another current concern is that, if we permit children to speak in their home-based languages or encourage the expressions of their cultural perspectives, our nation will become a group of ethnic enclaves rather than a united country. As a matter of fact, in many predominantly White junior high and high schools across the country, students of color *are* spending much of their free time with other people who look like them. They talk about this tendency as a way of surviving in a place where they are not truly wanted. White students also spend most of their time with other White people, but, ironically, this is seen as people spending time with their friends rather than "segregating themselves." The trend of students of color connecting most closely to others in their racial groups has prompted a great deal of debate about how the students in racially and ethnically diverse schools are "resegregating" themselves; those who worked hard for integration of schools particularly struggle with this issue.

Teachers frequently talk about their feeling that they weren't prepared for teaching in today's school environments. Perhaps that was what the student teacher meant by her comment about "emotional risk." Regardless of where we teach, I believe we will have to deal with issues that probably weren't included in our teacher education courses. A teacher in Texas said to me, "Some of my children live in dumpsters! No one talked about that when I was learning to be a teacher." A teacher in California told me that there were 22 languages spoken by children in her classroom. "How," she asked, "am I possibly supposed to be able to meet children's needs in their own languages?" The fear being expressed here is, "How can I do it? How can I fulfill my responsibility to see that children learn?" We often don't trust ourselves when we feel we don't have concrete information. In many ways, each of us needs to be given new tools, certainly new information; we need examples of how to be firmly committed to multicultural education and we need to be willing to live with uncertainty and discomfort. But the difficult truth is that we have to figure out much about teaching as we go. And the good news is that in many states, as in California, teachers are being given opportunities to retool, to learn how to respond to the additional requirements for teaching at this time.

Another complicated piece of the current early-education picture is that, not only are teachers working with varied groups of children, they are also teaching with much more diverse groups of colleagues, all of whom bring with them their own cultural approaches to education. In one child-care center with which I work there are three older women working as assistant teachers in classrooms. All of them have only recently come to this country so they are steeped in their respective cultures. One is having difficulty choosing "appropriate" ways to discipline children. When she was little, she was punished by being made to kneel on the floor in piles of beans or rice with her arms outstretched for long periods of time. Telling a child to "use your words" doesn't feel firm enough to her. The second new immigrant was asked by the director to come into the office. The director simply wanted her to sign a form; the teacher was terrified that she had done something wrong and was sure that she was going to be fired. In her country, she told the director, people only see the person in charge if something is very wrong. The third assistant teacher was quite put off on her first day of work when she wasn't fed before the children. In her culture, people her age are the most revered and, as a symbol of respect, are fed whenever they are hungry.

If we were using "old" recipes for responding to these three situations, we might have done any one of a number of things. We might have discounted any or all of the women as "from the old school," or "from the old country," or just for being "old." If we had taken the first one seriously, we might have worried that she would be too severe with the children and have watched her carefully. We probably would not have stopped to wonder what experiences with authority the second woman had had. We might have been outraged that the third woman wanted to "take the food from children's mouths." If we go back to our goal of keeping our minds and hearts open and being willing to listen *and* to change, we put our values and beliefs, our ways of doing things, on the table and work to come to a place where each and all feel valued. I hope we would stop to ask the woman who had been punished what that experience was like, what she had learned, and then talk about ways to help the children take their misdeeds seriously without physically harming them. We might look for ways to interact with the second woman that would not frighten her, but would reinforce the work she was doing. In fact, had the director known how the woman would feel about coming to the office, chances are good that the director probably would have taken the form to the classroom for her to sign. Finally, if we work to keep our hearts open, rather than thinking the third woman was out of line for wanting to be fed first, we might have thought about what it would be like suddenly to lose that status. In fact, we might have served her a bit of food first or offered her a plate with the children. It seems a small thing to do.

This is not about giving up our basic values or those things we prize most highly. If we're working with people whose cultural values are in conflict with ours, the challenge is to be willing to enter into dialogues in which *all* parties are willing to change. If we are able to maintain a sense of equanimity, to iden-tify the contradictions and not back away, and to see teachers as colleagues and not as competitors, the possibilities of moving to a different place togeth-er are good. We won't always feel understood, and we definitely won't always get our way, but by meeting each other face-to-face we offer other adults and the children with whom we work a model for a different way of learning.

ALWAYS BEING A LEARNER

The last element of laying our personal groundwork for participating in edu-cation that is truly multicultural is powerfully expressed in a statement attrib-uted to Rainer Maria Rilke (1875–1926): "If the angel deigns to come it will be because you have convinced her, not by tears, but by your humble resolve to be always beginning: to be a beginner."

This is a deceptively simple task: seeing ourselves, always, as learners; working with children, parents, and other teachers and staff with an attitude of humility and cooperativeness. It is so difficult to keep remembering how very little we know—especially when we are in the business of education. Yet it is a terrific strategy for success in working with others, particularly those who are different from us. If I am genuinely always a learner, acknowledg-ing that I don't know something becomes simple. If I remember that my experience is only that—my experience—I am more likely to listen to oth-ers' stories without judging. As a White person who grew up in the South, whose family is in the cotton business, and whose life's work deals with racism, humility is a necessity for me. At any moment I can do something that reminds me (and those around me) that my "White blinders" have gotten in my way; I am forgetting that some people have life experiences dramatically differ-ent from mine simply because of skin color. Similarly, as one who is "tem-porarily able-bodied"—as the community of people with disabilities calls those of us who still have relatively full use of our bodies—humility is crucial. In a literal heartbeat I, too, could be among those who navigate our com-munities in wheelchairs, are unable to feed or dress themselves, or are unable to see and/or hear. Such understanding helps keep my arrogance at bay.

There are other instances in which I think humility serves us well. I believe that we should enter into our relationships with the parents of our students humbly. So often we think, "We're the teachers; we're the ones who know. They are lucky to have us." But part of our responsibility to the children we serve is to support and cooperate with the parents as well. Humility and always being a learner are effective ways to connect with other staff members as well. When working with children, parents, and staff whose experiences are different from ours, who might be of different color or have disabilities, we must remember that we are the beginners—that they, in many ways, are the teachers and we

are the learners. By making it clear that we all have millions of things to learn, we provide an opportunity for others to admit that they are learners as well.

The exercise Diversity Questions for Educators in Figure 3.4 offers a great opening for dialogue about what you do well, what you wish you did better, and what all of you might learn together. Even though this activity was designed to use in thinking about your work with children, it could be easily adapted to apply to your interactions with parents as well as with staff.

While it is clearly an emotional risk to invest yourself fully in exploring your attitudes and behaviors, consider the alternative. If we are unconscious about our biases and prejudices or are in denial about the existence of racism, sexism, homophobia and heterosexism, class and physical ability discrimination, our relationships with others cannot be honest or whole. Creating a learning environment that is truly multicultural requires ongoing, intentional work on ourselves and the willingness to enter into that process with others. In order to avoid being like the child care-center teacher who washed her hands after touching Black children, we must commit ourselves to the risk of finding out if our behaviors match our intentions.

Figure 3.4 *Diversity Questions for Educators*

---

1. What are my expectations for students from diverse backgrounds? How do I communicate with them? At my institution, is it assumed that some children will be less "successful" based upon their backgrounds? What are my assumptions? What is the reality?

2. Have I ever been in a situation in which I made a comment or engaged in a behavior that I thought was perfectly innocuous but was considered sexist or racist by a child, a parent, or a staff colleague? How did I deal with the situation? What was the effect of this episode on me and others?

3. How do I deal with quiet or silent children? How do I deal with loud children? What assumptions do I make about their abilities and attitudes? Do these assumptions differ for White children and children of color? For boys and girls?

4. Do I call on or pay attention to girls as frequently as boys? Do I pay as much positive attention to students of color as I do to White children?

5. If I have language arts and math groups, how do children get assigned to the groups? Is there any relationship between what group the children of color are in and their participation in class? What messages are sent to the children by the composition of the groups?

6. How do I introduce discussions about issues of difference in the classroom? Am I comfortable enough with the issues to use the "teachable moments"?

7. Is there a pattern in the kind of children I encourage to assume responsibilities and take risks? Does my classroom reflect the style, comfort level, and interaction patterns of one particular culture or of many different cultures?

8. Do I consciously vary my teaching styles and instructional strategies in order to meet the different learning and cultural styles in my class?

9. What assumptions do I make about student aptitude, potential, skills or achievement based upon the child's cultural style, accent, or verbal skills?

10. In what ways am I conscious or unconscious of how my own preferences and subjectivity might reflect some race, gender, or cultural bias? These may relate to:

    a. encouraging students to take risks and assume responsibilities;
    b. expecting gratitude for my efforts;
    c. paying special attention to children, making them my favorites or "pets";
    d. giving open, straightforward feedback to children; and
    e. evaluating achievement and projecting achievement expectations of children.

Talking with Parents
About Multicultural Education

The tension in the field of early childhood education about cultural inclusivity seeps into any consideration of what "good" programs for children look like. How best to approach parents[1] about multicultural education and work with them on the issues involved is an additional concern. The ramifications of both questions are extensive and often feel daunting. In this chapter we will look at some elements of both of these problems and at strategies for responding to them. Again, there are no absolute answers or easy fixes, no cookbooks to turn to for tried-and-true recipes. The teacher's challenge is to ask better questions, ask them of more people, and genuinely and respectfully listen to their answers in the process of creating a multicultural classroom.

There is a broad spectrum of thought about the best way for teachers to work with parents in creating a positive multicultural learning environment for children. At one extreme is the model of teachers designing the classroom experience as they see fit and telling parents what is going to happen. This is the traditional line of thought in which there is a clear distinction between professionals and parents. At the other extreme is the

---

[1] Throughout this book, I use *parent* to mean the significant caregiver in a child's life. This could be a mother, a mother and father, a father, brother, sister, aunt, grandparent, or anyone else who has primary responsibility for the health and well-being of a child.

view that parents have the right and responsibility to determine what their children learn, how, and when. Somewhere in the mushy, as-yet-unclear middle is the belief that teachers must be very conscious of the groups with which they are working and plan accordingly, remaining in dialogue with everyone along the way. Seeing parents as allies and not competitors of teachers is important. The we're-all-in-this-together philosophy is the goal. Regardless of where we stand on involving parents in creating curricula, a continually reexamined theory is an essential foundation for our actions and behaviors. What each teacher needs is a belief system based on theory and experience and the willingness to reexplore all assumptions, thoughts, and concerns.

Building a multicultural curriculum with your students' parents is one of your most delicate responsibilities. Because none of us is free from prejudice, parents' biases, both about people who are different from them and about what school should look like, will probably crop up. If you are prepared for these responses, you will be less likely to be thrown off balance and more likely to listen with compassion. Attitudes about race and the other issues of difference are so complex and so deeply embedded that a great variety of responses from parents is possible. Reactions may range from the very positive to the highly negative. There are some things you can do to increase chances of creating a multicultural environment that you and parents both support: First, build strong relationships with the families of the children in your school or classroom; second, continue the ongoing process of examining your own biases and attitudes; and, third, create strategies for addressing both the concern about what to include in the curriculum and how to involve parents. Above all, remember: If parents know that they are able to be a part of their children's education and that they and their perspectives are respected, the elements of successful interactions are in place.

BUILDING RELATIONSHIPS WITH PARENTS

Working with parents is part of the teacher's job. Because a child spends so many hours in school, education is most effective when parents and the teacher act as partners in the child's development and learning. While the teacher's immediate job is to work with children, a vital element of the work is making connections with the children's families—making them feel included and an integral part of the classroom. Because multicultural education "permeates the physical environment of the classroom, the curriculum, and the relationships among teachers, students, and community" (Nieto, 1992, p. 215), the relationship that is created between parents and the school is crucial for helping parents embrace the educational process.

Making connections with parents is not always easy; cultural differences often add to this initial strain. In some situations the teacher and parents don't share a language. While this isn't an impossible barrier, communication is obviously more complicated, and everyone has to work harder to make him- or herself understood. Culture also manifests itself in attitudes about gender roles. There are cultures, for instance, in which men refuse to deal with female authority figures, and therefore the father of a child in the classroom won't talk to the teacher because she's a woman. While not a cultural difference, work schedules sometimes compromise a parent's ability to be involved in his or her child's school experience. For parents who work night shifts and sleep during the day or those who work 14-hour days, coming to a school event is often a luxury they can't afford. In cases such as these, the teacher should go out of her or his way to make connections as simple as possible for the parents.

White teachers are frequently surprised at the hesitancy with which Black or Hispanic or Asian or Native American parents approach them. Teachers usually see themselves as caring, unprejudiced people who welcome the children and parents, regardless of color, into the classroom. A White teacher needs to remember that, historically, people of color in the United States have not been treated well. This is not to say that White teachers need to be bound to this history by guilt. Rather, it is important to know of the actions of many Whites in the past and then to examine your own actions to determine whether you are doing all you can to work against the continuation of white supremacy. It is also important to be aware that, while the White teacher may not feel that she or he has personally discriminated against people of color, parents may be suspicious of the teacher, based on their experiences with other White people. In addition, White parents are sometimes hesitant about teachers who are people of color. We live in such a segregated culture that White people frequently have little personal interaction with non-White people, particularly people of color in professional positions. Again, both patience and understanding of the parents' reservations are important. It is essential that we be aware of the cultural histories that parents bring with them so that we do not have unrealistic expectations of establishing instant rapport and trust.

There are many things a school can do to strengthen the parent–school bond. In the situation of the father's not wanting to deal with a female authority figure, the teacher can bring in a male colleague to participate in the first few conversations. This helps ease the father into understanding that it is in the best interest of his child for him to work with the teacher. For all parents to feel welcomed at the school, a variety of ways for people to be a part of their children's education is important. Some schools and child-care centers have established school-related groups in which parents can participate in social and recreational activities; they choose topics for speakers and parenting classes they are interested in. One of the goals is that they get to know one another better so that a school community forms. Around the country, men's involvement groups are forming to bring fathers, uncles, older brothers, and grandfathers into the school environment and help them feel less peripheral to child care. Parents need to feel welcome in and knowledgeable about their children's schools. When possible, family members should be invited to participate in field trips, go on picnics, or stop in for a quick breakfast with the children on their way to work.

As parents and teachers get to know one another as individuals, trust builds between them, and school becomes less intimidating. Many cultures see schools and teachers as authority figures and therefore unapproachable. Frequent interactions between families and teachers are essential in building a feeling of trust. In addition to being together for parent–class outings, real relationships are built on

> equality in the parent–provider relationship [and] joint decision-making in matters affecting child and program, and mutual support that includes trust and celebrations of each other's contributions to children's development.... Inclusiveness requires genuine collaborations that transcend limited partnerships involving "we–they" approaches to the parent–program relationship. (Powell, 1994, p. 179)

Ideally, there is a context of trust and collaboration in which the teacher can initiate conversations about a multicultural approach to education. Even if that trust is not yet built, by the teacher's taking the families' cultural perspectives into account when the curriculum is being designed, parents become a part of what is going on. Another way of including parents is thoroughly discussing the curriculum with them. Because multicultural education brings to adults' minds the sensitive and emotion-laden topics of race, ethnicity, culture, gender, class, and sexual orientation, it is important that teachers communicate the goals and purposes of this approach directly with parents. It is also essential that teachers are willing to listen to parents' fears and concerns about these issues.

As I have stressed several times, teachers' understanding the complexities of their own attitudes helps them be open and honest with parents about the curriculum and less judgmental about parents' responses. Thus effective interaction about education that is multicultural requires that teachers be always in the process of examining their own attitudes and values about issues of difference. In other words, teachers cannot raise parents' awareness about injustice and inequalities if they are not exploring their own attitudes in this area.

EXAMINING OUR ATTITUDES TOWARD FAMILIES

While we have talked in Chapter 3 about examining our attitudes that are race-, gender-, age-, physical ability-, and sexual orientation-related, we have not mentioned teachers' attitudes about parents. Again, we bump into our culturally constructed pictures of what *family* means, of what good parents look like and how they raise their children, of how concerned parents participate in their children's lives. If to us *family* means mother, father, and two children, we might make negative judgments about other family configurations. The single-parent family might not look "whole" to us. In fact, we may be so stuck in our own picture of family as to call these "broken" families, thereby sending the message to the child that something is wrong with his or her home environment. If families of other patterns—two mothers or two fathers; or a mother, a grandmother, and an aunt; or two grandparents—don't seem "right" to us, chances are very good that we will treat the children of those families in a less positive way than children from nuclear families. Even if the configuration feels "right," the teacher's racial or ethnic assumptions can have an impact on how she or he interprets a situation.

For example, an African American child in a preschool setting was identified as having behavioral and learning problems. All the people involved in the assessment were White, including the school principal, the counselor, the psychologist, and the child's teacher. The parents attended conferences but were experienced as "hostile" by the teacher. After reading a report written by the psychologist saying the roots of the child's problems lay in the fact that he wasn't getting the support and structure he needed at home, one parent came in to talk to the teacher. She was obviously very angry.

> He [the psychologist] doesn't know what he is talking about. I'm the child's aunt, not his mother. My husband and I rescued the child and his two brothers from their mother, my sister, who is drug-addicted and was abusing and neglecting the children. My husband and I both took on extra jobs to support the three children, and we're doing the best we can. There was so much damage done by the time we got the children that we have lots to make up for. (Anita Schriver, personal communication, February 27, 1995)

The teacher reports that this woman broke down her assumptions and stereotypes. She thought she was dealing with a hostile and uncaring mother, but really the woman was an extremely caring and competent aunt trying to save the lives of the children. Too often our blinders get in our way of seeing all the possible scenarios.

Each culture has, at some level, a picture of what makes a "good" parent. Some believe that "good" parents keep their children in close physical proximity and encourage them to be very dependent for several years. Others believe that independence is an extremely important quality for young children to develop and do a great deal to encourage autonomy. Neither view is "right" or "wrong"; they're just different. But, if teachers are not conscious of their own biases on the subject, they will make positive judgments about parents who believe in one approach and negative assumptions about parents who believe in the other.

Finally, most cultures have beliefs about how parents should participate in their children's lives. Middle-class mainstream America has watched the Andersons in "Father Knows Best," the Cleavers in "Leave It To Beaver," the "Brady Bunch," and the Cosbys devote much of their time to the ins and outs of their children's lives. One of the strong messages being sent in all of these programs is "This is how good parents parent." In other cultures, such as in the kibbutzim in Israel, children are raised in groups and form attachments to several adults rather than just their parents. In German culture, "the ideal is an independent, nonclinging infant who does not make demands on the parents but rather unquestioningly obeys their commands" (Grossmann,

Grossmann, Spangler, Suess, & Unzer, 1985, p. 253). Teachers who are aware of the cultural effects on their perspectives and of their own cultural and racial biases have a better chance of being able to see a child or family accurately, rather than as what she or he assumes the child or family to be.

STRATEGIES FOR DEALING WITH PARENTS

After working to create a foundation of trust with parents and looking at your attitudes and assumptions about families, it is helpful to think about strategies for moving forward. We need to determine how, when, and if to include parents' cultural values and beliefs in the curriculum. We also need to consider ways of presenting multicultural education to parents and receiving their feedback.

Encountering Dilemmas

Many dilemmas arise as teachers struggle with building a multicultural curriculum. How, for example, does a teacher balance the diverse desires of parents, some of whom feel that the school program is too academic and others of whom believe that it is not academic enough? How does a teacher respond when a parent tells her or him that her child wouldn't be so out of control at school if the teacher would hit him when he was bad as she does at home? If a teacher has many different cultures represented in her or his class, what are the best ways to be inclusive? What if cultural beliefs about appropriate "boy behaviors" and "girl behaviors" clash? If there are several languages spoken in the neighborhood of the school or center, how might you shape it to be a place that really reflects the community? How do you deal with the issue of religion and the school so that you are being culturally sensitive while not supporting one religion or another? These are just a few of the questions teachers must grapple with, and the list is overwhelming. "I'm supposed to think about all of these things and teach children to read, too?" Yes, and more. Let's look at ways to address three of these questions.

• *How does a teacher respond when a parent tells her or him that her child wouldn't be so out of control at school if the teacher would hit him when he was bad as she does at home?* As is made clear in the exercise Exploring Your Own Ethnicity and Culture (refer to Figure 3.2), our beliefs about disciplining children are strongly affected by our cultural messages and our experiences. The ways in which our parents disciplined us were probably much like the ways our grandparents dealt with our parents' negative behaviors. We would probably respond similarly to our own children's acting out. Not only do we carry conscious or unconscious cultural messages, we also carry enormous negative judgments about people who see the subject (whatever it happens to be) differently. For example, both the teacher and the parent are clearly frustrated with the child's talking back to the teachers at school. The parent's assessment of the problem is clear: "He behaves for me at home because he doesn't want to be hit. He is out of control at school because he knows you won't hit him." Even if the teacher had been raised in a culture that spanked or hit its children, most, if not all, child-care licensing agencies forbid hitting a child while she or he is in the school's care. So the parent's solution is not an option. Further, many teachers believe that hitting children simply reinforces the message that hitting solves problems, so she or he wouldn't consider that approach anyway. The task for the teacher who wants to be respectful of the parent's culture and experience is to find a way to arrive at a middle ground with the parent. The teacher might ask the parent about her or his goal in hitting the child. Chances are good that the parent either wants the child to stop a behavior or to understand its seriousness. The parent and teacher might agree that the important thing is for a behavior to be discontinued or the point to be made. Their job is then to figure out what other approaches they might use to stop the specific action. While we don't know exactly what they will come up with, the process should be to talk about what each adult wants the child to learn and what each of them can do to support the other's way of helping the child learn without compromising their most closely-held values.

• *What if cultural beliefs about appropriate "boy behaviors" and "girl behaviors" clash?* I once taught a 3-year-old child we'll call Luke. He was a timid, mild-mannered, diminutive, African American only child whose mother was the primary caretaker. Luke spent most of his waking life at the day-care center. His mother dropped him off at 8:00 a.m. every morning. She then took a bus, two trains, and another bus to get to her job at the phone company. Every night she picked him up at 6:00 p.m. Left to his own devices, Luke would spend most of his day in the dramatic-play area, dressing up in dresses, aprons, and high heels, cooking and cleaning. Other children would move in and out of that area, but Luke stayed there. His other teachers and I weren't too worried; we believed that he was working on something and that, when he had finished, he would broaden his activities. (He did exactly that about two months later.) Usually, Luke had taken off the dress-up clothes before his mother arrived to pick him up, but one day she came early. She was furious that we let Luke wear women's clothes and demanded that he never be permitted to do it again. I talked about our philosophy of children's getting to make choices and not being caught in gender-role stereotypes and said, rather dogmatically, that if she didn't want him to dress up she would have to take him to another day-care center. I'm afraid my tone was "I'm the teacher, and I know best." The mother said she would think about it, took Luke, and went home. They were back the next morning at 8:00 a.m.; she never mentioned the incident again. I also changed my behavior; since I still believed that Luke was in the housekeeping corner for good reasons, I let him stay there. But, after nap every day, I suggested he do something else so that when his mother came she wouldn't find him dressed in women's clothes.

Hindsight is always 20/20, of course, but I do know that today I would handle it differently. I still believe that children should be able to make choices about their activities, and I still believe that boys should get to try on what it is like to be a girl, and vice versa. Today, however, I would stop to talk to Luke's mother, to hear what her concerns were, and try to figure out what we were going to do about the situation as a team. And I would have to leave open the possibility that I would change my handling of the event, or my part of the conversation would lack integrity. What I would probably do is suggest we talk together with Luke to find out what he liked about the housekeeping corner. I would also be interested in knowing if he was dressing up as a specific person or trying out being another gender. I would work to discover the root of the mother's feelings. This is not as simple a solution as it might sound. I am deeply committed to eradicating sex roles; I don't believe that gender (or race or culture, and so on) should limit anyone's opportunity to do anything. Women should be able to be President, and men should be able to stay at home and be artists; people should be free to choose. But I also know that if I dismiss someone else's perspective because it is different from mine, if I don't enter into dialogue with the parent, I won't have been successful in my work with the child or the parent.

• *How does a teacher deal with the issue of religion and the school so that she or he is being culturally sensitive while not supporting one religion or another?* This is one of the hardest issues to talk about, and I believe it is only going to get harder. Historically, we were a predominantly Christian country with communities of Jews scattered around the nation. There is now a rapidly growing number of Muslims and Buddhists in the United States, and their influx will certainly have an impact on teachers.

Most of us bring such emotion to the subject of religion that virtually no conversation is passionless, much less objective. The United States, at this point, is facing many court cases on prayer in the schools, the teaching of "creationism" rather than evolution, and the legality of using public-education vouchers to enroll students in private religious schools. *USA Today* reported on November 11, 1994, that 22% of all adults identify themselves as members of the "religious right." Religious-right coalitions are running people for elected office all over the country, many for local school boards. They were instrumental in removing the exciting and innovatively multicultural "Children of the Rainbow" curriculum from the New York City public schools because they objected to the inclusion of positive information on homosexuality (Berger, 1992). So what might have been simply an animated conversation at other points in history is now a deeply divisive one.

The answer (if there is one) to the question of being culturally sensitive to people's religious views without supporting religion is really about

being conscious of our behaviors. Obviously, conversations among the children about God or religion can and will take place. What is legally problematic is any breach of the separation of church and state as established in the United States Constitution. We also have to be careful how we step on people's toes without intending to: singing Christmas carols in school as if everyone celebrated Christmas; putting up Christmas decorations as if it were a cultural event rather than a religious one; ignoring religious dietary rules; setting up meetings on religious holidays or on Saturday or Sunday; being insensitive to children whose religions don't celebrate birthdays, like the Jehovah's Witnesses. This is a very thorny path, one we have to walk carefully.

Anticipating Responses

It is important for a teacher to understand both the positive and negative feedback to efforts at implementing a multicultural curriculum. Often, mainstream parents are very excited and grateful that their children are being prepared for life in a diverse world. They feel this part of the educational process will stand their children in good stead. Parents of color, gay and lesbian parents, single parents, or parents with physical disabilities may feel relieved to find themselves included in the curriculum when they are so often left out. Parents also might respond negatively to multicultural education for a variety of reasons. Some White parents may fear that they will be left out of the curriculum. There is a misperception that multicultural, anti-bias education is only for people who are "other" than White and middle class. Others may fear that "the basics"—reading and math—will be given short shrift if multicultural education is the focus.

> Given the recurring concern for the "basics" in education, it is absolutely essential that multicultural education be understood as *basic* education. Multicultural literacy is as indispensable for living in today's world as reading, writing, arithmetic, and computer literacy. (Nieto, 1992, p. 211)

The teacher who has anticipated the variety of parents' responses to multicultural education will be less defensive when talking with parents. For example, with a class composed primarily or exclusively of White children, the teacher could expect that some parents might not see any reason for a multicultural approach. In this case, the teacher may want to emphasize that the children's exposure to and understanding of different cultures is excellent preparation for living in our society which is multiracial and multicultural. It is a necessary part of any teacher's job to support children's growth as social beings, and a social being lives positively in a world composed of people who are like us and people who are different from us. The teacher might emphasize that failing to provide a variety of experiences would be *mis*educating children by leaving them ill-equipped to function in the world.

Some parents view a multicultural approach to their children's education as different from the education they themselves received and thus may feel it to be inappropriate. These parents may be suspicious of such an approach. If this is the case, you can stress the fact that through such a curriculum each child's self-concept is nurtured. Because the approach to multicultural education affirms individual differences, each child will know that she or he is special and valued. The multicultural educational process teaches children to be respectful—of themselves, of each other, of their similarities and differences. Often parents who have grown up in traditional American educational circles (along with a lot of the rest of us) are dismayed at the lack of respect we see children showing each other and the adults in their lives. Parents are, in general, pleased to have their children learning more about respectful behavior.

The most important strategy for presenting multicultural education to parents involves listening to their fears and prejudices in an accepting and non-judgmental manner. Making parents defensive and angry will not win their support for the curriculum. As teachers, we can ask the parents to talk about their hesitancies regarding the curriculum. Again, all of us have unresolved issues about differences. By really listening to a parent's concerns, we allow the parent an opportunity to examine her or his own feelings and fears.

Frequently this process of examination diffuses the parent's worries. As I have said before, teachers must deal with children's families respectfully, creatively, and compassionately.

Looking at a Model

Around the country there are schools that teachers, parents, and town residents have designed as authentic multicultural communities. I thought it would be helpful to describe one briefly as a way of looking at the role teachers play in the success of such a venture.

Several years ago, a public elementary school was founded in an urban industrial community on the East Coast. Through the efforts of teachers, public-school administrators, university supporters, and community members, the school was designed to create programs that mirrored the rapid population shift in the region from largely White to 25% Cambodian refugee and 25% Hispanic immigrant families. Care was taken to ensure that the school's policies and structures would be culturally responsive to the Cambodian and Hispanic families. Bilingual teachers were recruited so that parents and children could communicate in their home languages while they were learning English.

Organizing the school's programs into early childhood (PK–3) and primary (1–4) units prevented teacher isolation and encouraged teaching teams to plan, teach, support one another, and collaborate over the details of school and classroom life. Families and teachers worked together in a way that encouraged consensual decision-making among both individuals and culture groups. Respect for the children's home language skills led to providing rich language acquisition opportunities for all of the children. Five years into its operation, the school hums with conversation and instruction in three languages. Children and teachers have learned to shift easily between languages.

Diversity is woven into the fabric of the school. The children see adults from different cultural and language backgrounds work closely together. They know that almost everyone comes to the ice cream party, field day, and the pot luck suppers. They are included when teachers and families mingle at school gatherings. They see people laugh, tell funny stories, and have a good time together.

The lessons for other teachers from this experience are, perhaps, these:

1. Affluent members of the school community—whether teachers, administrators, or family members—must understand the difference between creating a multicultural program and doing charitable work. A school community is unlikely to evolve into a collaborative social organization if some members believe they are doing others a favor by participating.

2. Important cultural differences are likely to emerge among families and teachers, and these differences should be used to enrich discussion about education and child rearing. Some of these differences may affect people at profound levels and have serious implications for cross-cultural communication. For example, Cambodian families sometimes use a medical intervention called "coining," in which the edge of a coin is rubbed on the surface of the skin to stimulate circulation. Sometimes this results in noticeable bruising. Parents and teachers who are unfamiliar with the technique are likely to view it as abusive. School leaders should provide formal and informal ways of dealing with issues of this kind, rather than assuming that benevolent reactions will necessarily follow the decision to "respect cultural differences." The goal is to convey that there are many ways of responding to children that are in the range of "good teaching" or "good parenting."

3. Because communication is so important, anticipate what it will involve to translate school documents and messages into several languages. At the school in our example, considerable burden has been placed on bilingual teachers to deliver messages or translate written materials sent between school and home. If the budget allows, consider hiring part-time family liaison people. Otherwise, recruit community or parent volunteers for some of this work.

Though few of us have the support and resources available to this model school, many teachers around the country are dealing with children whose home-based languages are very different one from another. While the situation is not in your control, your response is. The goal is to design ways to include the children's language and culture daily so that parents feel they too have a place in their children's educational process.

Our success in dealing with the parents of any type or class depends on sensitivity to family needs and experiences, and basic respect for parents' ideas and values. The need for sensitivity and respect increases when dealing with the deeply personal issues related to diversity. We must work to learn about parents, their cultures, and their experiences. We must pursue getting to know the children and their families by asking about family histories and stories, by having a family guest day, or by inviting parents to come in and share information on something about which they have expertise. There is no end to ideas about how to make parents feel welcome and part of the school community, to make them feel valued for all of who they are. It is essential that communication lines between parents and teachers be strong and be always open. Regardless of points of view, if the parents and teachers stop talking to each other, the real loser is the child.

Preparing for
Multicultural Education
in the Classroom

Before attempting to create a multicultural curriculum or classroom environment, it is essential to have a theoretical foundation for your work. If you set a specific goal—a multicultural curriculum—and design objectives and activities and guidelines that support the goal, you are far more likely to achieve the classroom environment you want than if you simply put together a collection of activities. You are also better prepared for the inevitable "hard questions" that children and families ask about issues related to diversity. This chapter introduces two perspectives on multiculturalism to help you shape a theory on which to build a curriculum; it also offers guidelines for dealing with race in the classroom. Finally, a series of levels of involvement are suggested to help you measure your commitment to multicultural education.

THEORETICAL BASES FOR
A MULTICULTURAL PERSPECTIVE

Two contemporary theoretical approaches to multicultural education provide us with a foundation on which to base classroom and curriculum design. The first is Jaime Wurzel's (1988), and the second is that of Sonia Nieto (1992). Wurzel identifies seven stages of moving toward multiculturalism (see Figure 5.1).

Figure 5.1 *Stages of the Multicultural Process (As described by Jaime S. Wurzel, 1988)*

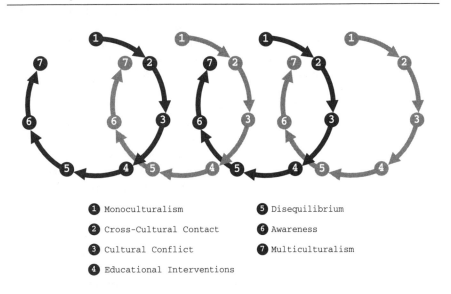

1 Monoculturalism   5 Disequilibrium

2 Cross-Cultural Contact   6 Awareness

3 Cultural Conflict   7 Multiculturalism

4 Educational Interventions

The first stage in this model is *monoculturalism*, in which each individual assumes that his or her culture is universal; it never occurs to her or him that there may be people who are different or other ways to live. Wurzel describes monoculturalism as key to ethnocentrism which, as we have seen, is the belief that one's own cultural group is superior to all others. This is the stage at which someone says, "Cultural differences don't really matter. We are all human beings with the same needs and values." Inherent in this stage is the sense that "All people see the world as I do, and, if they don't, something is wrong with them." The stage is *mono*cultural because individuals see only one culture. The ethnocentrism is so pervasive that people aren't even aware that there are people in other cultures who are equally as ethnocentric about their own groups.

At some point in most people's lives, information about other cultural ways creeps into their experience. It might be as minimal as contact with a different culture's foods or visiting an ethnic neighborhood at a time of a holiday festival. Wurzel calls this second stage *cross-cultural contact*. Although there is no real awareness, there is a dim perception that there are people other than "us."

Stage three is *cultural conflict*, which "is not only the clashing of different cultural patterns. It is also the confrontation of two or more ethnocentric views" (p. 6). Often the two sides draw their lines of separation even more clearly; the boundaries harden. Most young children are egocentric and ethnocentric by definition, that is, they see themselves as the center of the universe. The sun rises because they open their eyes; parents get divorced because of what the children did. Thus it is often difficult to sort out which part of a conflict is intercultural and which part is age-connected egocentrism. For example, it might look like this: Jacob, one of few young Jewish children in a school, and Evan, a Christian boy, get into an argument over Christmas. Evan asks Jacob how big his Christmas tree is. Jacob says he doesn't have a Christmas tree; he's Jewish. Evan replies that everyone has a Christmas tree and that, if Jacob doesn't, he's stupid. With children slightly older than preschool age, the conflict might go further. Evan gathers support from other children, taking a poll to prove that Jacob is the only one without a Christmas tree, and Jacob is left feeling isolated and alone. What makes it worse for Jacob is that each teacher in the school has put up a Christmas tree in his or her classroom, so that everywhere Jacob goes he is reminded of his difference. Part of the problem is Evan's egocentrism; part is conflict between cultures.

The fourth stage consists of *educational interventions*—a stage of getting new information. The new information prompts a transition from stage three, *cultural conflict*, to stage five, *disequilibrium*. Some educational interventions are intentional: "The Jewish culture is one I know nothing about. I had better do some reading." Some are not: "I just discovered that people in the United States knew all along that the Holocaust was taking place!" If we stay with the example of the two boys, Jacob and Evan, what happens in stage four is that through some process of education—a teacher reading a book about Hanukkah or a parent's comment that some people celebrate Christmas and some don't—Evan moves to the fifth stage, *disequilibrium*. Having believed that everyone celebrated in the same way his family does, he becomes confused and begins to struggle with what the truth is. *Awareness* grows (stage six), and Evan is on the path toward multiculturalism.

Because it is stretching Wurzel's analysis a bit to apply it to young children, let me give you an example from my own experience to show more clearly what *disequilibrium* means in Wurzel's model. While it is now difficult for me to believe, I had no close contact with Asian Americans, in particular Japanese Americans, until I graduated from college and moved to New York City in 1969. Even more surprising, I had never heard about the Japanese internment. However, I had begun to struggle seriously with injustices I knew had been inflicted on Black people and my own ancestors' participation in them. I had also begun to see some of what I perceived as hypocrisy in the notion of America as "land of the free and home of the brave." I realized that the extent of your freedom—to vote, to get a good education, to choose a restaurant in which to eat, or a church in which to worship—depended in large measure on the color of your skin. To apply Wurzel's model, by age 22 I had experienced some new cultural information and some cultural conflict.

But I was in no way prepared for an "educational intervention"—a visit to a photography show at the Museum of Modern Art in New York City. The exhibit, entitled "Executive Order 9066," was a collection of photographs showing Japanese people in California and other West Coast cities being herded from their homes, put in trucks, and taken to "internment camps" in the outback of the West. I felt pain, confusion, panic, disillusionment, and finally anger, at this exhibit. "Disequilibrium"—the losing of my balance—sums up my feelings. I felt confused and betrayed by my country. The Germans had had concentration camps, not us! Wurzel tells us that

> Disequilibrium in the multicultural process occurs when previously held knowledge is challenged or invalidated. At this stage, students begin to doubt and question some of their attitudes and beliefs. Hopefully, an inner emotional and intellectual struggle will take place. (p. 10)

While disequilibrium is not always as dramatic as my experience at "Executive Order 9066," there is always an element of internal conflict: "Before, this is how I perceived the world and truth. Now I am not so sure." Awareness is raised, the Piagetian process of assimilating new information takes place, and the thought systems change to accommodate the new knowledge.

These stages of the multicultural process frequently are not smooth; they usually produce a broad range of feelings and emotions; and, if the process works as Wurzel believes it does, we evolve into a greater understanding of the complexities of our world. And, as Figure 5.1 shows, we go through these stages many times in our lives. When I first realized that I had been lied to about Black people, I began to move through the stages Wurzel describes. I began again when my mother refused to travel through Europe with one of my best friends from high school who was Jewish. And again as I deal with my responses to the growing number of "street people" who beg in my neighborhood in Berkeley. Moving toward authentic multiculturalism is life-long work; we begin time and time again. What the smooth circles in Figure 5.1 do not show is that it is a jerky, start-and-stop-and-start-again process. While it is not always something we really want to engage in, it is part of the emotional risk described in Chapter 3.

Sonia Nieto's definition of *multicultural education* shares some common themes with Jaime Wurzel's. As pointed out in Chapter 1, Nieto (1992) believes that multicultural education is a *process* by which change occurs; she underscores the difficulty of altering personal attitudes. *Reflection* and *awareness* are essential ingredients in multicultural education; unless each of us experiences some jarring of what we see as "normal," our ethnocentric perspective remains in place.

Nieto stresses that multicultural education is also *antiracist, antidiscriminatory,* and *education for social justice.* Essentially, her message is that teachers who practice authentic multicultural education must be willing to look at the ways in which different races, cultures, genders, ages, and sexual orientations add value to a school, an experience, a work place. They must also be willing to carry with them the recognition (as differentiated from guilt) of the terrible injustices that did and do go on, and that understanding must guide their teaching.

One of the goals of any preschool curriculum is to help the young child move from her or his sheltered family unit into a much more complex environment. Taba (1962) states that

> the curriculum should develop the knowledge and perspective which is commensurate with the kind of world in which we live, a world that…is composed of an unlimited variety of outlooks, backgrounds, and standards of living. (p. 213)

Preschool can be a step in socializing the child, in helping the child change from an egocentric, ethnocentric person to one who understands and is sympathetic to people of considerable diversity.

Wurzel (1988), Nieto (1992), and Sleeter and Grant (1994) agree that multicultural education is not something that can be grafted onto the curriculum. Working with children toward the development of positive racial attitudes and the affirmation of other differences is central to all stages of commitment to multicultural education. The Human Relations approach to Multicultural Education (Sleeter & Grant, 1994) is built on nurturing a positive self-concept for every child from the earliest years. These strong positive feelings about themselves should help children feel less threatened by change and by diversity.

As we see in other approaches that Sleeter and Grant (1994) describe, multicultural education is not solely concerned with developing good feelings of self in the children of color who are so frequently the victims of racism in the United States. Equally important is the positive depiction of White male and female heroes who have worked to bring about change in the United States and in the world. Thus a classroom that reflects a multicultural perspective is a supportive environment in which children of all races can grow. It is also a place in which they begin to learn about social justice in ways that are appropriate developmentally. Integral to this approach is commitment to broadening children's awareness and valuing of diverse cultural heritages and experiences, as well as the teacher's pledge to continue to "be a beginner."

SOME SPECIFICS TO CONSIDER

There are obviously some ways in which the racial or ethnic composition of a class affects the techniques a teacher selects to use in exposing young children to cultures that are new to them. There are not, however, as many variations as one might think. The main one is that in a heterogeneous class one is able to draw on the experiences of the children rather than having to "import" diversity, relying solely on visitors, pictures, and books. For example, if there are Spanish-speaking children in a primarily English-speaking class, the children who speak English can learn Spanish words and phrases from the Spanish-speaking children, and vice versa. Children love to know more than one name for an object or a variety of ways to say "Good morning." Teachers in a heterogeneous class have the luxury of being able to choose from a collection of ways of doing things, such as cooking or playing games, that come directly out of the class community. Teachers in a homogeneous class, on the other hand, must provide a hypothetical multicultural community for their students. Even in a biracial class, however, it is important for children to see that there are other people of color in the world besides those represented in their class.

With encouragement to explore, to initiate activities, and to make the classroom work for them, children are active participants in their own development and learning. In an environment rich in diversity, children are able to experience a variety of people, objects, and situations. By playing games, cooking foods, or singing songs in ways that children from other cultures do, young children begin to see that people who do things differently are not frightening or wrong. Rather, learning new games or songs from children of other cultures makes life more interesting. By building on young children's own experiences, teachers can provide them with new activities that expand their understanding and with experiences that enable them to identify with and care about people of diverse backgrounds, values, and lifestyles.

However, because the young child is developmentally so egocentric, it would be inappropriate to barrage her or him with too much specific information about cultures and countries totally foreign to her or his life. For example, to a young child it seems that the cave people, dinosaurs, and Great Grandmother Margaret all lived at the same time. For most children who live in Topeka, a trip to Kansas City is the same in terms of distance as a trip to Puerto Rico: You get on a plane or in a car and go and go and go. Unless children have a way to connect personally with a geographical location and go there repeatedly, they are not likely to understand distances or different countries. Regardless of where the classroom is—in a large, diverse urban community or in a homogeneous rural or suburban community—young children need to encounter diversity without too many confusing specifics. For instance, by including carefully selected pictures of Eskimo, Latin American, Asian, and African people on class bulletin boards, without talking directly about Alaska, Latin America, Asia, or Africa as geographical and cultural entities, a teacher lets children know there are all kinds of people in the world. At the same time, this does not confuse children by giving them information too unrelated to their own situations.

It is important to note that some books and materials, such as pictures of American Indians in feather headdresses or Inuits going to hunt for seals, can reinforce stereotypes, so it is crucial that teachers be very selective about the materials they display. Here is an example analyzed in terms of Wurzel's seven stages of multiculturalism. A teacher of 5- and 6-year-olds wanted to teach her class about Native American cultures. She had probably moved beyond Wurzel's first stage, monoculturalism, to the second stage, cross-cultural contact, because she already realized that her own culture, Irish American, was very different from Native American cultures and that the children would benefit from knowing more about American Indians. She gathered a variety of materials—a drum, a teepee, a clay pot, and several eagle feathers to use in headdresses—and brought them into the room. A Native American parent, whose child was in another class, was quite distressed when she saw the feathers. Eagle feathers are sacred to many tribes, and it is wholly inappropriate for a non-Native American to use them or for them to be used other than in religious ceremonies.

At this point the teacher moved into stage three, cultural conflict. From her perspective, she was "trying to do something multicultural." From the parent's point of view, the teacher was being insensitive, and the parent went to talk to the principal. The principal brought the teacher and parent together to try to smooth things over, and a difficult conversation followed. The teacher said the parent was "being too sensitive"; the parent said the teacher was being "racist." Each left angrier than she came in. After a short cooling-off period, the teacher and the parent decided individually that they didn't really want to leave things as they were.

The teacher began to do some reading and research, moving into Wurzel's fourth stage, educational interventions. While she learned a lot, the reading was also confusing. She realized that her education about Native Americans had been filled with faulty information and stereotypes. She became more aware of her lack of information about tribal customs. Many books talked about Plains tribes, yet showed pictures of Pueblo Indians. Women were spoken of as "squaws," men as "bucks." The "good Indians" were the ones who helped the White people. She also read horrifying stories of how the Native Americans were treated by Whites, herded onto reservations, lied to and tricked, and whole tribes destroyed systematically. Somehow, the history she had been taught had been sanitized so that these behaviors didn't sound genocidal. This stage, disequilibrium, was uncomfortable, but in the process she felt that she began to learn how to teach the children about Native Americans using real information rather than stereotypes. She moved into awareness, stage six, and closer toward real multiculturalism.

The Native American parent also learned a lot as she progressed through the stages. She grew more compassionate toward the teacher who was, in fact, the only person in the school who was trying to teach anything at all about American Indians. And she decided to bring some clay pots and Zuni fetishes for the teacher to use in her display. She also agreed to work with the teacher and the children on other Native American projects for the class.

Not all stories end as positively as this one. Each woman had hit a sore spot of the other's. For many White people, being called a "racist" is incredibly hard. For a person of color, being told you're "too sensitive" is extremely painful. Here, both the teacher and the parent were willing to admit that they each had something to learn. The teacher could have stayed in stage three, cultural conflict, and never moved on. Instead, she took a closer look at herself and decided that perhaps the parent was right about her unconsciously being insensitive. The parent recognized she could use an ally in the school and that probably this teacher was her best choice. The key to the relatively happy ending is that each had motivation for moving through a tough process. No one can make us change; we have to understand that it is in our best interest to do so. The payoff, however, is enormous. We continue to learn about ourselves and other people. Furthermore, the relationships we build with people who are different from us are based on a foundation of growing honesty which, in turn, builds trust.

GUIDELINES FOR DEALING WITH RACE IN THE CLASSROOM

Whether or not a teacher has planned a curriculum that focuses on race and cultural differences, classroom conversations about racial issues often arise. These can be difficult to address. In some ways, such conversations are more important than planned discussions because they frequently spring directly from the children's concerns, from things they have noticed in the class or in the world around them. Young children, as has been mentioned, are aware of race and concerned about racial issues by the time they are 4 or 5 (Derman-Sparks, Higa, & Sparks, 1980; Goodman, 1952/1964; Morris, 1981) and often ask questions about differences or express their confusion. To approach impromptu conversations about race or other differences most effectively as a teacher, you may find it helpful to do some internal preparation by considering what your responses might be to the children's remarks. If you are in the process of becoming comfortable with discussing sensitive issues, spontaneous comments are less likely to throw you off balance. While doing the internal work necessary for such conversations is not an easy task for any adult in our society, it will be very difficult to encourage positive feelings about differences in the children if you are ill at ease yourself. What follows are some situations that other teachers or parents found themselves in and how they responded or might have responded.

- A class of 3-year-old White and Asian children and their two teachers were taking a walk. On seeing an African American mother and little girl coming toward them, an Asian child said very loudly, "Look, Jane, it's a little Black girl." One of the teachers reported that she prayed that the pavement would open up and that she and the whole class would disappear, but, since this didn't happen, she had to respond. Her first impulse was to shush the little girl, but she realized quickly that the discomfort was basically hers. She looked at the Black mother and daughter and smiled, and said to the Asian child, "Yep, that's right." The conversation ended and the child went on to another subject. Had the scenario been different and involved a person in a wheelchair, the same response would have worked, but it would have been a good idea to follow up on the conversation later with the children. "What did you think when you saw the man using the wheelchair?" "Do you remember seeing a person in a wheelchair before?" "I wonder why he's using the wheelchair." The same tack is possible with a child who comes to school and says, "My friend Esther has two mommies." Probably the best response is, "Oh, that's interesting. Tell me more about it." The point here is not to overreact or to project your feelings of discomfort to the child or children. A matter-of-fact response allows the child to continue with her or his thought processes without getting caught in yours.

• The next one is not so easy. A young White boy was riding in the grocery cart his mother was pushing. They turned into a new aisle and came upon a Black mother and daughter. The White boy looked at the Black child and said to his mother, "Look, Mom, it's a baby maid!" What really happened is that both mothers kept walking straight ahead, acting as if nothing had occurred. Several years later, the Black mother repeated the story and asked what advice I would have given to the White mother and what advice I would have given to her. There is almost nothing the White mother could have done to ease the discomfort. It is a nightmare. But two things are important for the White mother to do: to acknowledge to the African American mother that it happened, and to take responsibility for her child's behavior. A possible scenario might have been for the White mother to look directly at the African American mother and say, "I'm really sorry. The only Black person he knows is the Black woman who works for us." That communicates to the African American mother that the White mother is conscious and caring, and that is about the best she can do. The primary concern of the African American mother would be for her child. And the message she would probably want to send is, "People sure can say dumb things." The task is to reassure the Black child that the *other* child is confused.

• A White single mother had a biracial child whose father was African American. The child looked a great deal like his father and had very dark skin. One day the son asked, "Mom, when I grow up will I be White?" This, like the "baby maid" story, is actually not far-fetched when we look at how many young children think. "This is what grown-ups look like, so, when I grow up, that's what I'll look like, too." Or, "I've seen a grown-up one of these so this must be what a little one looks like." The question "Mom, were you Black when you were little?" is exactly the same, only reversed. Young children speak only from their experience; it makes sense that they generalize from what they know directly.

The teacher can plan to initiate discussions about race instead of avoiding them. You can deliberately find occasions to talk about such things as skin color, hair, and the other physical characteristics that can distinguish different races. One way to do this is by introducing new materials. For example, you could read a book to the children about a Chinese American family and then talk about the appearance of the characters in the book. "Do the people in the book look the same as the people in your family or in our class? In what ways? How do they look different?" Cultural differences can also be explored. In previewing a book before reading it to children, look at how the characters do things. How do they greet each other? By hugging, by kissing, by bowing? What sorts of traditions are presented? Do the characters sleep on beds or on mats on the floor? What do they eat and with which utensils? Obviously, not every book will provide a possible conversation about "the ways people do things." You can, however, periodically choose books that give you openings for such conversations.

If a book or material contains racial stereotypes, you should not ignore them but should find a place for them in the discussion. For example, after reading a book that portrays a traditional White nuclear family with mother at home and father out at work, include in your conversation about the book, "We know something that the person who wrote this book doesn't seem to know. Not all mothers stay at home while fathers go out to work," or "Not all of our families look like the one in this book." At the least, it is crucial to have books and other materials that depict the experiences of each of the children in your class. It is even better to have stories about a very broad range of people regardless of the class composition. Biracial and multiracial children, for example, often feel left out. Children in stories are either White or African American, Latino or Japanese American. If you have children in your classroom who are Vietnamese and African American or White and Chinese American, it is very important to include materials that look like those children. If you cannot find them, take pictures of all of the children in the class and of their families and make books using the pictures. In this way both the children's life experiences and respect for differences in general can be validated and supported.

Another way to initiate discussions about differences is by talking about the physical characteristics of the children themselves. (Obviously you want to guard against falling into the ever-present trap of being overly concerned with how people look, but the concreteness of an individual's physical attributes is useful for young children.) This is particularly helpful in a classroom that is racially mixed, but it is possible to do it in a homogeneous classroom by talking about differences in hair color, eye color, height, and skin color. Conversations about physical characteristics can be interwoven throughout a day. "Look at Yuan Lee's beautiful shiny black hair." Or "Keisha, your braids are wonderful. Your grandmother must have worked hard last night." Or "Caitlin, your hair gets blonder and blonder the closer we get to summer. You must be spending a lot of time outside." Or "Look at how you are all different heights. Let's make a wall chart showing how tall each of you is, and then we will check in three months to see if you have grown taller." Rather than being an "add-on" to the curriculum, it is organic as it comes from what the children themselves bring.

The more comfortable you are with racial issues yourself, the better you will be able to respond to children's questions and racial concerns in a straightforward and easy manner. Information should be given to young children simply, without so much technical detail that the children become confused. For example, in a racially diverse class a boy named David asks, "Why am I Black and Jane White? I want to be White so I can be like Jane." There could be all sorts of things behind this seemingly simple comment: "Why do some people have one color of skin and some have another?" "Why am I different?" "Why is she different?" It is important to stop and ask why the Black child wants to be like the White child. Probably the most pressing concern for a child lies in the question about being different, so a long discussion about skin pigmentation, melanin, and its role in determining skin color is inappropriate and unnecessary. I once saw a teacher try to explain the whole concept of melanin to a group of 3- and 4-year-olds. She went through quite an elaborate process, and at the end one of the children said, "You mean we have different colors of skin because some of us eat more melons? If I eat a cantaloupe or a piece of watermelon, will my skin get darker?" More to the point would be a brief explanation: "Some people have more melanin in their skin than others, just as some people have black hair and some have red hair." (You could try "skin pigment" instead of "melanin," but my hunch is that the children might think you were talking about pigs.)

The teacher could address the second question by asking David why he would like to be like Jane. At the root of the question may be a simple desire to be like a friend, or it may be the Black child's feeling or observation that White children are the ones who are in more books, or are happier, or have more toys. If the child does seem to feel that being White is better, the teacher could talk with him about his perceptions of how skin color makes a difference in a person's life, asking such questions as "Do you like being Black?" "Why or why not?" "Why would you want to be White?" Through such discussions children can begin to explore their ideas about skin color. These beginning conversations are important because they give children, regardless of color, permission to talk about their confusing feelings about race and color of skin.

I don't want to ignore our feelings as adults when we hear children of color make self-deprecating remarks. I recently had a conversation with a biracial (African American and White) mother who is married to a White man. Their 4-year-old daughter is having a hard time with her own slightly dark skin and even more trouble with the mother's darker skin. The little girl talks constantly about how she doesn't like her mother because she is Black; she refuses to play with her Black dolls. At school, other children make negative comments about blackness and the teacher does nothing to stop them. I was overwhelmed with sadness and anger at the thought of a mother having to know that her child feels such things. Before I could offer any guidance to the mother I had to acknowledge what was going on inside me. Though it might not be appropriate to express our feelings to the parent or child, if we forget to take the step of recognizing what we're feeling, at least to ourselves, our responses might carry inappropriate affect.

Opportunities regularly present themselves for conversations about gender as well. Even in the mid-1990s, stereotypes have not changed as much as some of us would have liked. Too often, in my experience, comments about "girl things" and "boy things" are heard in the classroom. "You can't play with us. You're a girl." "Girls can't be truck drivers." "You be the nurse. Doctors are always boys." "You can't wear that dress [or be a dancer or play with dolls or stay at home and cook]; boys don't do that." The role of the teacher in these situations is to be clear about what can happen in the classroom or school and at the same time not make judgmental comments about what the rules are in the child's home. "In this class, we don't divide what people can do by whether they are boys or girls. All children can choose the activities they would like to be involved in." If a child then says, "But at home my mommy has to cook. My dad says it's not his job," the teacher's best response is, "Sometimes things are different at home than they are at school. Here you can choose." You might also hear a girl say, "I wish I were a boy." It is important in a situation like that to find out what the child means. As was mentioned in Chapter 2, Ann Beuf (1977) found that Native American children repeatedly demonstrated that the reason for preferring a White doll over a Native American one was that Whites have easier lives, both socially and economically. It would make sense that girls might express a desire to be boys, not because they don't like being girls but because the options for males are so clearly broader than they are for females at this time.

Slurs of all kinds need to be dealt with directly when they arise. Just as it is not okay to call someone a "spic" or "slant-eyes," it is also not permissible to call someone a "fag" or a "sissy" or "fatty" or "cripple." There are three steps to dealing with slurs at school, whether in the classroom, on the playground, or in the cafeteria. First, ask what is going on: "Jeanine, what is going on between you and Jose?" After hearing the specifics of the disagreement, ask the child what she or he thinks the word used means. Often, young children are parroting something someone else has said and have no idea what the word actually means. They usually do know that the word will get a response. After the child responds, you can ask why he or she called the other child such a name. You might then talk about the word, perhaps following Wilson's (1980a) suggestion about dealing with someone being called "nigger":

> If children want to know what the word means, they should be told the truth:
> "It is a word that used to mean the color black. It came to be a word that means

Black people. For a long time now it has been a word that means Black people are not as good as Whites. It is a word that hurts." (p. 18)

If you are not clear what words mean and why they might be hurtful, do some reading so that your response is heartfelt and clear. Words have such power that we need to know what we are saying and what we are hearing. "Fag," for example, is short for "faggot." Faggots are sticks and branches tied together to use as fuel for a fire. In the Middle Ages, homosexual men were tied together and burned, much as if they were sticks. "Redskin" is an American term created in the late 1600s and early 1700s to identify American Indians. White people hired bounty hunters and paid them for each Indian they killed. The proof was to bring back a square of red skin from each Native American they murdered. Most probably, you will not want to give young children the gruesome origins of these words, but, if you understand the viciousness of the language, your comments to the children will probably be clearer. The most important message you can give children about slurs is that it is not acceptable to use them—that they hurt people and make them feel bad.

Since it is probably not developmentally possible for most young children to empathize with others' feelings, they cannot fully understand the power of slurs. It therefore does little good to say, "How would you feel if someone called you a _____?" The best way to deal with slurs, after asking what provoked the name-calling and then discussing what the word means, is simply to say, "In this classroom, calling people 'nigger' (or 'honkie' or 'spic' or 'fag') is not okay. You may not do it." If the child then says, "But my father calls them 'niggers,'" you can say, "Yes, some people do, but in this classroom it is not all right." By handling the issue of the parent's racial attitudes in this way, you let the child know that some things might happen at home which are not accepted at school and vice versa, rather than asking the child to choose between parent and teacher.

LEVELS OF INVOLVEMENT IN MULTICULTURAL EDUCATION

The last aspect of preparing for multicultural education is assessing the level of commitment you have made to it. Because each teacher has different skills, teaching situations, and life experiences, it would be unrealistic to expect every teacher to bring the same talents or the same commitment to developing multicultural education for her or his students. While some teachers may be ready and able to redesign their entire programs to reflect a multiculturalism, others may not be sure how it relates to them and their teaching. Nieto (1992) believes that there are at least four levels of development in working toward multicultural education: *tolerance; acceptance; respect;* and *affirmation, solidarity, and critique.* Why is it important that there are different levels of involvement? As discussed at the beginning of this book, we are on a journey—nationally, professionally, and personally. None of us has arrived. Exploring different levels of attitudes, behaviors, and commitment to becoming more multicultural (or more anti-bias or anti-racist) allows us to see where we are on this journey and what we need to focus on in order to move forward.

Tolerance, as Nieto sees it, is the act of "enduring" but not necessarily "embracing." It is the lowest level of commitment to multicultural education. We are often tolerant of things we don't really like, but have to live through anyway. If someone says to you, "I'm tolerating the cold weather," there is nothing that suggests enjoyment or pleasure. To tolerate people who are different is to put up with them, even though you would rather not: "We have to do African American History Month—if we didn't, they would think we were racist." If you find yourself having such feelings, examine the roots of your irritation. Is it that you feel you are being forced to do something you don't want to do? Are you resentful of the pressure not to look "racist"? Do you feel you are ill-equipped to do a good job on a curriculum related to women? To move beyond this level, you might begin to do some extra reading on people who have had different experiences from yours. Begin to listen genuinely to the parents of color as they talk about their struggles with racism. Compassion for others often moves us beyond tolerance. Once we begin to make connections with others, we see that it is in our best interest, and in the interest of the children and families with whom we work, to move to the next level of multicultural education.

Acceptance has a very different feel from tolerance. When you are at the level of acceptance, there is a recognition that multicultural education is an important goal even if you do not know exactly how to get there. To be successful at this level of involvement, you will begin to reassess your curriculum to see how it can become more inclusive. It will be clearer to you that involving parents in the educational process and taking their cultural beliefs and values into account are essential to creating a good learning environment for the children. You will begin to develop more and more activities that are multicultural. Children will receive messages many times a day that there is a variety of ways to do almost everything and that doing things differently is fun. "This week we will eat with chopsticks; next week we will try cooking only foods we can eat with our fingers." "Our families look different: some have one mother; some have two fathers. But they are the people who love us." When you find yourself at this level, begin to identify other ways to bring issues of difference into the classroom.

While acceptance is certainly more positive than tolerance, there is still a certain reluctance to embrace fully people who are "other." The families in your classroom will feel far more valued for who they are if you are able to move to the next level, *respect*. To Nieto *respect* means "to admire and hold in high esteem" (p. 277). At this level, the children and their families know that they are central to the school community. They come together for school events (if at all possible) because they know that their involvement is part of what makes the school experience good for their children. If you are at the level of respect, you will work to create an environment in which it is safe to talk about racism and the other "isms"; there are reflections of a commitment to multiculturalism in every aspect of the school day.

The highest level in Nieto's paradigm is *affirmation, solidarity, and critique*. Two elements make this level very different from the others. First, there is no part of the curriculum, the school day, policies and procedures, staffing, and interactions with parents and children that is not suffused with multiculturalism. Each child's home-based language is part of the curriculum; the families' cultural values are an integral part of the school's way of doing things. There is an understanding of how institutional racism, sexism, heterosexism, and so on manifest themselves, and there is ongoing work to combat each of them. The second element that separates this level from the others is the willingness to enter into conflict with one another and the commitment to work it through. Any time cultures come together in genuine ways, conflict will arise. Nieto (1992) quotes Mary Kalantzis and Bill Cope:

> Multicultural education, to be effective, needs to be more active. It needs to consider not just the pleasure of diversity but more fundamental issues that arise as different groups negotiate community and the basic issues of material life in the same space—a process that equally might generate conflict and pain. (p. 277)

Unless adults are willing to be real with each other—to express what we hold most dear, knowing that others may be holding on to something diametrically opposed—we cannot truly affirm others and stand in solidarity with them.

The *affirmation* level is a destination, not a stopping place, for many of us. It is something I have been working *toward* all my life. I have a hunch that it will always be a goal for me. To reach this level requires consistently looking for ways to go deeper into ourselves, our biases and prejudices, and our privileges. We must also go wider; it is not enough to work on just race or only on gender. The motivation is to build whole relationships with people who are different from us. It is also essential that we model those behaviors for the children and parents with whom we work.

As you think about the four levels identified by Nieto, try to place yourself in one of them and see how it fits. Think about why you put yourself there and if that is where you want to be. If you are satisfied with that level, ask yourself why. If you are not, think about what you need to do to move to the next level. For example, if you place yourself at the level of *acceptance,* think about why you are hesitant to adopt a stronger stance on multiculturalism. Explore times at which you felt uncomfortable with someone different and why those times had such strong effects. If you want to move forward but do not know how, identify what enabled you to move from tolerance to acceptance. With this sort of self-study, it is likely that you will be able to reach your desired level of commitment to multicultural education. As you engage in this process, talk with others who teach with you regarding the level all of you want for your classroom and for your center or school.

Planning a Unit on
Affirming Cultural Diversity

$\mathbf{I}$n Chapter 5, I stressed the importance of building all curricula, and a multicultural curriculum in particular, on a strong theoretical foundation. I have chosen to include a unit in this chapter because the actual way a unit is structured forces us to think concretely about a theoretical matter. In other words, to create a successful unit you have to know where you want to go and why. The process of designing a unit helps you figure out how to get there.

Teaching a unit is an opportunity to devote some focused classroom time to multicultural education. While there should always be a variety of activities that incorporate the goals of multiculturalism, when teaching a unit the materials and experiences are presented within a specific time frame. The approach is more thorough and organized in that each experience the children have builds upon preceding experiences and suggests future experiences. For example, the children might visit an ethnic grocery store to buy the ingredients to make a particular recipe when they return to the classroom. That activity might be part of preparation for fixing lunch for another class.

The unit is an organizational structure you use to ensure a balanced, integrated presentation of materials and information to children. It should be emphasized that the unit is a tool for you, not for the children. In planning a unit on any subject, you identify ideas, skills, attitudes, and values that are integral to a particular concept that you would like the children to understand. You then design learning activities that support a concrete exploration of the concept at a level that is experientially, culturally, and developmentally useful for the children (Taba, 1962; Taba, Durkin, Fraenkel, & McNaughton, 1971). While most young children will not be able to understand the values and attitudes or the concepts and ideas in the terms in which they are stated in this unit plan, it is hoped that they will assimilate the values into their own developing value systems and will grasp some of the basic ideas as they participate in the activities.

Most young children are, as has been said, egocentric and ethnocentric; they see themselves and their own cultural groups as the center of the world. As they develop, their focus begins to broaden to include other people. It is crucial for young children to see that there are many kinds of people in their community and that these differences are part of what makes the community interesting. In order for children to affirm diversity in cultural heritages or life-styles, they must have opportunities to experience alternative ways of doing things and opportunities to share with and learn from people who are different from themselves.

This unit was developed to provide a multicultural perspective for young children. It focuses on Native American, Asian American, Hispanic or Latino, African American, and White people as part of a total community.

UNIT PLAN

Main Idea

Many different cultures work together and contribute their unique qualities to form a strong community.

Organizing Ideas

    A. There are many different kinds of families.
    B. All kinds of people live in our community.
    C. There are some ways in which we all are alike.
    D. There are some ways in which we are different.
    E. We work together in our community.

Skills to Be Developed

In the context of the unit, the children will have the opportunity to develop and use the following skills:

Observing	Differentiating
Comparing & contrasting	Working together

Describing	Defining
Generalizing	Gathering information
Developing concepts	Hypothesizing
Predicting	Explaining
Sorting	Classifying
Solving problems	Offering alternatives
Matching	

Attitudes and Values to Be Developed

- We are all innately, inherently worthy. Our worth is based on ourselves, not on someone else's worthlessness.
- We are all born equal but not the same, worthy of respect and dignity regardless of color, gender, culture, sexual orientation, or physical ability. Our capabilities are based on our individual drives, desires, opportunities, and education.
- We need to value and affirm differences. Each of us is unique and special. Our differences, when joined together in a common task, give our group strength. We grow and learn from experiencing and working with each other's differences and from finding commonalities.
- Each of us is an important individual. At the same time, we are all valued members of a group. If we work with other members of our group we can frequently be more effective than if we work by ourselves.
- The concept of change is a positive one. Although all changes are not necessarily positive, the concept itself is one to be valued.

Organizing Idea A. There are many different kinds of families.

Learning Activities

1. Begin by asking the children about their families and who they live with. As they tell you, make a chart using markers (one representing a dog, one a mother, one a brother, one a grandfather, and so on) to show how many people are in each family.

   Talk about how people form family groups: children are born to parents, children are adopted, people come together out of love and necessity.

   Read a book with the children that talks about the fact that almost everyone has a family, but there are lots of different kinds of families: mother–child; mother–father–child/children; grandparents–child/children; mother–mother–child/children; grandparents–parents–child/children; father–father–child/children; older sibling(s) caring for younger children; extended families including aunts, uncles, cousins in the primary group;

and so on. There are also families in which there are no children. Include them in your list of families as well. Remember to include family pets.

2. Provide magazine pictures of a variety of people. Find examples of people resembling family members of the children in the class, such as grandmothers, aunts, cousins, mothers, fathers, siblings, and pets. Ask the children to build the portrait of a family using the magazine pictures. The children will probably base their pictures on their own families. Display all of these pictures, at the children's eye level, in the group meeting place.

    Make a list with the children about what they see in the pictures. How do all of the people look alike? How do they look different?

3. Find lots of pictures in magazines of all kinds of families; mount and laminate some and put them on the wall or bulletin board, at the children's eye level, for them to look at and enjoy. Include all major cultural groups and all sorts of family configurations. Since one of the goals of this unit is to broaden children's experience and knowledge, intentionally include multi- and biracial families and families with lesbian and gay parents. Mount and laminate other pictures and use them in group discussions and various learning activities. For example, ask children to find the family with two sisters, or with a father, or with younger parents or older parents, or with a grandmother and grandfather. Through such an activity children will become aware of the wide variety of families.

4. Provide a blank book for each child to use in writing a story about his or her family. Since the children are not yet able to read or write, they can dictate stories to you. Encourage the children to put whatever they want to about their families in their books, for example, stories about deaths, divorces, and births, as well as everyday occurrences.

5. Make a new-word chart of words children use to describe how their families look, what they do, and so on. (Even though the children are unable to read, if they help you put the words on the chart and look at it every day, they will soon remember the words. Part of pre-literacy is learning that the spoken word can be written down.)

6. Take the children on a trip around the neighborhood. Let them show their friends where they live. Show them where you live. Talk about who lives in each child's house or apartment. Talk about who lives on their blocks. Do old people live on the block? Are there lots of children? Ask them what sorts of buildings, stores, animals, people, and growing things they saw on one block that they did not see on another. Make a list of what you are seeing as you go.

    Take a camera with you and photograph the children's houses. Also use the camera as a "traveling camera" for parents to take home to photograph their families.

After returning to the classroom, make a language experience chart about the trip by writing next to each child's name a comment by the child about the experience. Using the list made on the trip, count how many dogs or grocery stores or stop signs were seen. Ask the children to dictate stories about the trip.

7. Invite the children to build the neighborhood with blocks. Put labels on the buildings, including a sign showing where each child lives.

8. Ask how the adult members of the children's families spend their time. Make language experience charts listing this information.

    In order to support all children's life experiences, remember that parents or other family members who are not working outside the home are doing useful things at home, such as housework and caring for children. Include these jobs in the language experience charts.

9. Repeat the above activity, focusing on how children spend their time. Do they have jobs in the classroom? Do they have jobs at home?

10. Choose a few books that show people playing and read them to the children. Select ones that you think mirror their own experiences. Provide opportunities to talk about how people in different cultures play differently. (For background information about play, see Roopnarine, Johnson, & Hooper, 1994.) What do the students do with their whole families? What do they do alone? What do some family members do together that is special? For example, grandparent and child walk to school each day, brother and sister build forts together, mother or father and child work in the garden or play in the park.

11. Ask the children what songs their families sing together. Let them teach the songs to the other children.

12. What kinds of routines does each family have? How are these routines alike from family to family? How are they different? How are the routines like the ones at school—for example, brushing teeth after meals and setting tables?

13. Ask the children what their favorite foods are. Locate recipes of the children's favorites. If possible, have parents come to school to cook with the children. How are the foods that the children eat at home different from one another? How are they alike?

    Compile a family cookbook to which everyone contributes a favorite recipe.

    Invite families to eat breakfast or lunch with the children. Let the children cook for the families, using recipes from their recipe books.

14. Put out the people block accessories in the block corner. Make new family block accessories by attaching a magazine picture or a photograph of a person to an appropriate-size block, making sure that you have multicultural, nonsexist accessories that do not reinforce racial or gender stereotypes.

15. Make simple graphs about the number of children in each child's family, number of pets, number of adults in each family, number of boys, number of girls, and so on.

16. Change the housekeeping area so that it represents various kinds of homes, by putting up new curtains, various pictures on the wall, and so on.

    Have a wide variety of dress-up clothes available for the children: various ethnic clothes, various occupation-related clothes, clothes that parents might wear, clothes that grandparents might wear. (Since dramatic play provides an opportunity for children to try on a variety of roles, all children should feel free to wear any of the clothes regardless of the sex roles or genders suggested by those garments.)

17. Provide materials for the children to use in drawing or painting pictures of their families. An older child might enjoy stitching a simple family sampler that she or he has designed.

18. To consolidate this part of the unit, review with the children the work that they have done on families. Do a language experience chart that will help you assess what the children have learned about how families are the same and how they are different.

    Make a big mural or collage using pictures of various kinds of families that the children find in magazines or draw.

19. To begin the transition from families to people in the community, talk about how all of the children's families together form a group of people—people who live together and work and play together, people who are all part of the same community.

Organizing Idea B. All kinds of people live in our community.

LEARNING ACTIVITIES

1. To acquaint the children with the concept of community, draw on the work that has been done on families. Point out that family members all do their parts to keep the household running, just as each child in the classroom does her or his job to see that everything is taken care of at school. A community is a group of people who live near each other and can work together in ways that are helpful to everybody.

   Have the children look at the mural or collage they made toward the end of their work on families. Point out to them that the people whose pictures are on the mural form a community.

2. Make a cozy area in the room in which children can sit quietly. Put up pictures of people from a large variety of cultures, being sure to include pictures of people of all ages. Put pillows in the cozy area to encourage the children to sit and look at the pictures.

3. Make a mobile of pictures of children's faces, representing many cultures. Hang the mobile so that the children can see it while they are in the cozy

area. Ask the children how the people in the pictures on the wall and in the mobile look different from each other and how they look the same.

4. Talk with the children about who lives in their communities. They will probably mention a variety of community workers as well as their own families and their friends' families. Make a "People in Our Community" language experience chart listing all the community workers, being careful to use nonsexist terms for the workers, such as *police officer, salesperson, firefighter, mail carrier,* and *newspaper carrier.* Put pictures by some of the names of the community workers. As the children meet more people in the community, add their names or functions to the "People in Our Community" language experience chart.

    Invite the children to dictate stories about the jobs of the community workers and to illustrate their stories. Combine their stories and make a class book. (See Learning Activity 7, below.)

5. Take trips to see people who work in the community. Include in your selection of community workers members of a variety of ethnic, racial, and cultural groups, women and men. In addition to having the children find out what these people do, talk with them about how each of these people helps the whole community run more smoothly. If the class is unable to take trips to see community workers, invite workers to the classroom to talk with the children about their jobs.

6. On trips around the school neighborhood, note how many businesses are in the community. (If your school is isolated from the center of the

city, visit the central business district, if possible.) Take pictures of the stores and the buildings.

In the block corner, encourage the children to make a simple model of the business district of their neighborhood. The first step in this process is to make a language experience chart or write stories about the neighborhood the children visited. Put the pictures you took of the buildings up on the wall in the block corner, at the children's eye level, so that the children can use them as guides for their buildings. (Four- and 5-year-olds who have built in the block corner a lot should not have any trouble with this task. Younger children or children who have not built much will have to simplify the task to suit their building skills.)

7. Ask the children to keep a book on "People in Our Community." This can be a class project with each child contributing a dictated story, or children can make their own books.

8. To begin the transition from talking about community to talking about ways in which people are all alike, ask the children to name all the people whom they have put on the "People in Our Community" language experience chart or about whom they have dictated stories in their community book. Get them to think about ways in which all these people are alike: they all wear clothes, they all eat food, they almost all live in houses or apartments, they all work, they all play.

Organizing Idea C. There are some ways in which we all are alike.

LEARNING ACTIVITIES

These activities focus on five ways in which all people are alike:

We all eat.
We all work.
We all play.
We almost all live in some sort of dwelling.
We all wear clothes.

The essential ingredient for this section of the unit is lots and lots of pictures. Photographs that you have taken of the children can be supplemented by pictures from your file that focus on people of all colors, shapes, and sizes. In most instances you will want to mount the pictures on poster board and laminate them, but it is a good idea to decide which activity you are going to use each one for before mounting it since you may want to color-coordinate a group of them for a specific learning activity. Choose pictures that show one of these five categories: people eating, people working, people playing, clothes people wear, or people's dwellings. When choosing magazine pictures of dwellings, use those that are not so different from the children's experience that they take on a "foreign" or "exotic" air.

1. As a way to prepare for this section of the unit, take as many snapshots as you can of the children in your classroom and others in the school eating, working, and playing. Focus some of the pictures on the clothes that the children are wearing. Also photograph dwellings in the school's neighborhood and the students' homes. You might also take photographs of people using tools or doing things that the children could replicate using similar items.

2. To introduce this part of the unit, show the children a collection of pictures of all kinds of people eating, working, wearing clothes, playing, or living in their respective dwellings. Talk to them about what the people are doing. Provide opportunities for children to try the things they see happening in the pictures. Ask questions about the pictures, taking care to point out things the children might have missed.

3. Make a sorting game using two to five pictures from each of the five categories listed above. Make a big pocket-chart out of fabric or a set of manila envelopes pasted onto poster board and put picture and word labels under each pocket; for example, the label could say, "We all eat," and on the label would be a simple picture of a person eating.

   Explain the game to the children: "Sort the pictures by putting each one into the pocket where you think it should go. Look at the pictures on the labels to tell you what group of pictures goes in each pocket. When you have finished sorting, we will talk about how you chose which pocket to put each picture in. Lots of the pictures could go in more than one pocket."

4. Make matching lotto games using pictures of dwellings, people eating, or clothes people wear.

5. In the block corner put up pictures of various sorts of dwellings and encourage the children to build structures like those they see in the pictures.

6. Put books in the quiet area that deal with one or more of the ways in which we are all alike. (See Appendix B for suggestions.)

7. Make puzzles for your manipulative-materials area that are related to one or more of the five categories. Pictures can be glued to cardboard, laminated, and cut into sections or strips for the children to reassemble.

Organizing Idea D. There are some ways in which we are different.

The purpose of this section is to help children understand that there are some things we all do but the ways in which we do them vary according to what we learn in our families. Children will begin to get a sense of cultural heritage and its effects on our actions and our approaches to the way in which we live our lives. Since cooking, music, and holidays are outward signs of the basic values, rules, and belief systems inherent in each culture, looking at them provides children with concrete clues about what cultures value.

LEARNING ACTIVITIES

These activities focus on five areas in which people do things differently:

> Cooking
> Making music
> Carrying out a daily routine
> Talking together
> Celebrating a holiday

Introduce this section by sharing with the students several books showing children of various cultures doing the things listed above. Ask the children what is happening in the books. Ask if they have ever done what the characters in the books are doing. Let the children share their experiences with you. When possible, do the activities they see in the book.

Cooking

1. Make a cookbook with the children adding these recipes to the collection begun in the first section of this unit.
2. Each cooking experience should begin with a trip to the grocery store, if possible. Two or three children and a teacher can make the shopping list, buy the ingredients, and bring them back. Letting the children help buy the foods not only gives them a better sense of what the cooking process involves but also gives them the opportunity to see where food comes from before it gets to their homes.
3. Ask family members to cook with you and the children or to join you when the children are cooking something new.

Music

1. Teach the children all sorts of songs, and let them teach songs to their classmates.
2. Listen to music from various cultures. Sing songs, play records and tapes, and take children to neighborhood musical events. Use these experiences to help children identify and label the feelings that music inspires, such as joy, peace, and excitement. Encourage children to move with the music, clap hands in time to it, use rhythm sticks along with it. Tap out a rhythm and invite children to repeat it, using hands, feet, or sticks.
3. Introduce to the children new musical instruments from various cul-

tures. Instruments such as reed pipes, bongo drums, castanets, or maracas are interesting and enjoyable.

Daily Routine

Even our simplest actions, such as many of our daily routines, reflect our cultural heritages. The order in which we eat our food, the ways we hold our eating implements, when and how we bathe, and how we wash, dry, and fold clothes are all partially shaped by our cultures. Thus it is important for teachers to be sensitive to their own ways of carrying out daily routines as well as being aware of the children's ways of doing things. For example, many White middle-class Americans set a table by putting the fork to the left of the plate and the knife and spoon to the right, while some Puerto Rican people set the table the opposite way. In our ethnocentrism, it would be all too possible to think that the Puerto Rican child who set the table with the fork on the right and the knife and spoon on the left was making a mistake.

1. Begin thinking about daily routines by revisiting the messages you received about how meals take place in families. Does everyone sit down together? Does everyone eat the same food? Are children expected to use "good" table manners and what does that mean to you? (For example, can children leave the table during meals or do they sit with the adults throughout the meal?) Is the table set in a particular way? If so, what does the setting look like?
2. After raising your awareness of your cultural biases regarding "proper" behavior at meals, ask the children to talk about their families' meal times. Talk about what they eat and with what implements. Begin to introduce different eating implements to your class if the children are physically able to handle them.
3. Make a chart of the foods that children eat in their homes, being *very* sensitive to the fact that how much money a family has greatly affects what they eat. (Set up the situation so that, no matter what children mention, there won't be any value judgments from you or the other children.)

Talking Together

The ways we speak and the languages we speak are largely determined by our cultural heritages. Because of their egocentricity and ethnocentricity, young children who speak English in this country never think about the fact that not everyone uses English as her or his first language.

1. Find books that are written in two languages, such as *Moja Means One: A Swahili Counting Book*, by Tom Feelings, and *Abuela*, by Arthur Dorros. (See Appendix B for other suggestions.) Read them to the children.

Talk about the language in the books; ask them to listen to the sounds of the words. Ask them if they can understand the words in the new languages. How does it make them feel not to be able to understand the words?

2. If you are fortunate enough to have one or more children in your classroom who speak a language other than English, be sure to encourage the English-speaking children to try to learn that language, too. In this way the English-speaking children come to understand how difficult it is not to speak the primary language, and the non-English-speaking children have the satisfaction of sharing the ways in which they communicate within their own culture with their English-speaking friends.

Holidays

I am of several minds about the celebration of holidays in the classroom. My basic belief is that the less made of holidays the better. *I am not suggesting that there should be no celebrations in the classroom. I think celebrating with the children is important, but those events should come organically out of the children's school experience.* For example, if you plant a garden, celebrate planting the carrots by reading *The Carrot Seed*, by Ruth Krauss, and having a feast of carrots.

The problem comes with trying to recognize all of the holidays celebrated by the myriad cultures in the world. First, a school can't possibly celebrate all holidays, and clear messages are sent by what is included and what is excluded. If you celebrate Chinese New Year but not Tet, for example, are you implying that the Chinese are more important than the Cambodians?

Second, I am a strong believer in the separation of church and state mandated in the United States Constitution. Even by celebrating Christmas in a public school we cross the line between religious and non-religious. Christmas is a *Christian* holiday, not a cultural one, just as Easter is. Saint Patrick's Day is fuzzy; it is definitely an ethnic holiday—Irish—but at the same time it is also a Roman Catholic feast day. Because the United States is a predominantly Christian country, those of us who are Christian see our holidays as part of the culture. For those who are Jewish or Muslim or Buddhist and do not celebrate Christmas, that time of the year can be painful. Many Jews have talked about experiences of being teased or treated thoughtlessly by people who assume that everyone celebrates Christmas. Simply walking into a shopping mall reminds Jews that they are different.

Third, I have seen far too many preschool curricula that have holidays as their central focus: they begin the school year with Halloween, then move to Thanksgiving, then to Christmas. The new year focuses on Valentine's Day, then St. Patrick's Day, then Easter, and then school is out. But it is by looking at our *daily* life that we truly understand how our cultural differences play out. The celebrations are the *special* times where the differences have a distorted importance and we move into what Louise Derman-Sparks (1989) calls the "tourist approach."

Fourth, in my experience, the celebration of holidays often supersedes or even masks ethnocentrism and racism in the school and in the community. The notion is that, if we all sing songs and celebrate together, we are a happy family. The issues of power, discrimination, and historical and current racism are swept under the rug, following the theory that if we don't talk about them, they won't exist.

Having said all that, I also know that my perspective reflects that of maybe 5% of the country's educators. I was referred to by one child-care center with which I worked as "the Grinch who stole Christmas." Since the other 95% of people who work with children want guidelines for dealing with holidays in the classroom, here are some ways to approach the complicated subject of holidays that may prove helpful.

Historically, schools in the United States have fallen into an ethnocentric trap regarding celebrations. Only recently have schools begun to celebrate holidays other than the ones promoted by White Christians. However, although most 3-, 4-, and 5-year-olds cannot really understand the concept that people live in other countries, they are able to understand that some people celebrate Christmas and some celebrate Hanukkah.

Taking a multicultural approach to the issue of holiday celebrations requires two primary commitments: to celebrate holidays honored by various cultures, giving them equal importance in the curriculum; and to provide children with simple, honest, historical accounts of the bases for these holiday celebrations. For example, on Columbus Day *don't* tell the children Columbus discovered America. He didn't. Tell them he was a famous explorer who sailed across the ocean from far away and landed at a place which later was called *America*. Be sure to tell them that when he arrived there were Native Americans who had been living in "America" for a long time.

One way to approach holidays is to encourage parents to take the initiative if they wish to celebrate, in the classroom, holidays cherished in their cultures or families. Have as one of your ongoing themes "Families." That focus provides opportunities for all parents, grandparents, or other family members to visit the school or to organize a special event for the students, teachers, or for the entire school community.

Have non-traditional celebrations at traditional holiday times. For example, around Halloween do a unit on masks, remembering that, for very young children who aren't yet able to separate reality and fantasy, masks are often terrifying. At Thanksgiving, celebrate "Harvest" or "Bread and Soup" to honor the community feeling.

Julie Bisson (1992) developed the following guidelines for implementing holidays in anti-bias early childhood programs. For further discussions of culturally diverse holiday celebrations, see Ramsey (1979) and Derman-Sparks (1989):

1.   Decide on the underlying goals for holidays in your curriculum. Answering "why?" precedes decisions about what, when, and how. Consider the reasons for celebrating holidays in relation to the staff, children, and families, as well as the anti-bias goals.
2.   Develop a holiday policy that outlines how holidays will be used in the program. What role you want holidays to play in the program, how many holidays you want to celebrate, how much time you want to spend celebrating holidays, how you will make decisions about which holidays to celebrate, and how to involve parents and other staff are just some of the topics to consider.
3.   Decide which holidays will be celebrated in your program.
   • Develop a draft list of holidays staff members think are important to celebrate.
   • Find out what holidays are important to the families in your program.
   • Identify holiday activities that are expected of your school/center and community.
   • Consider the pros and cons of introducing holidays of cultural groups not present in your classroom.
   • Decide if there are holidays you want to avoid or downplay.
   • Consider inventing your own special days or rituals that become part of the culture of your classroom.
4.   Plan how you will celebrate each holiday while being consistent with your holiday policy and goals for celebrations given who the children in your program are.
   • Consider the developmental abilities of your children.
   • Pay attention to the balance between holidays and other components of the curriculum.
   • Decide how you will address the religious beliefs and content that are at the core of many holidays.
   • Make a plan for avoiding a "tourist approach" to diversity when implementing holiday activities.
   • Identify what stereotypes are present in each holiday you have chosen to celebrate and make decisions about how you will deal with them.
   • Plan how you will meet the needs of children in your program who do not celebrate holidays (Jehovah's Witnesses, for example).
   • Plan how all staff and parents who want to can be involved.

Organizing Idea E. We work together in our community.

This is the culmination of the unit. The purpose of the section is to help children see that we are all alike in some ways but our differences make us unique and special. If we work together and share those unique characteristics, we can learn from one another and grow with one another.

LEARNING ACTIVITIES

1. Make a class book. Include in it a collection of the children's dictated stories and pictures of people doing things with people of other cultural heritages.
2. Make a big class mural. Include pictures the children have drawn as well as photographs you have taken of the children as they have done unit activities. You might want to draw a life-size silhouette of each child, giving the children the opportunity to paint and decorate them. When the mural is finished it will be an example of what gets done when all of the children work together.
3. Review the unit with the children and talk about the activities they have done. Make a language experience chart with dictated descriptions of what they remember about the activities.

4.   Look at the stories, murals, and the work that took place during the unit
     to see if you think the children understood its basic goals. What aspect
     of the unit did the children like best? What part did they least enjoy?
     What will you change the next time you use the unit?

EVALUATION

Evaluation is the process by which teachers assess children's progress in their
work or their understanding of an experience, an idea, or a concept. Through
evaluation teachers can also measure the success of their own presentation or
organization of material or of a given lesson. Evaluation is an ongoing process.
In a preschool classroom the teacher constantly notes children's responses to
each other, to the teacher, to the work, and to the environment. Sometimes
this process is formal: teachers can identify the milestones in a child's growth
by recording observations and keeping records. Some of a teacher's evaluation
of a child's growth is informal: through interactions with the child or through
casual conversations with parents about how a child is doing at home, the
teacher gains information that reveals developmental changes.

The evaluation of the unit on affirming cultural diversity is similar to the
rest of the evaluation that goes on in a classroom. Formal evaluation includes
recording how children approach and work on suggested activities. Children's
verbal responses to questions concerned with cultural diversity or the nature
of their responses to people who are culturally different (both in and out of
the classroom) can help you evaluate the child's understanding of the unit's
ideas. Further, formal evaluation is built into the activities themselves. Since
many activities in this unit build on previous activities and prepare the children for future ones, you can evaluate your ordering of experiences by watching the children's reaction to each new activity. If the children are confused
or unable to contribute, you know that you must provide more experiences
at an earlier developmental level or in a different teaching style. Informal
evaluation takes the form of noting the degree of the children's involvement
in the activities. The combination of formal and informal evaluation can give
you a good deal of information about the success of the unit.

Because this unit is organized into sequential and related learning activities, each concept and idea is presented in a variety of ways. By using the
unit as a model for curriculum planning, rather than using a less organized
or structured approach, there is a greater chance that you will present the
values and concepts more concretely and they will be incorporated into the
child's thinking.

Seven

Developing a Multicultural Classroom Environment

Designing a multicultural classroom requires a very high level of involvement in multicultural education. At this stage, you are ready to adopt a multicultural perspective in all aspects of the curriculum, in the physical environment, and in your approach to the education of young children. Just as a curriculum reflects the system of values of its creator and of the culture of the children in the classroom, curriculum materials reflect the attitudes of the person or people who choose materials. The pictures on the walls, the books on the shelves, the dolls in the dramatic-play area, and the tapes in the music area in a classroom designed by a teacher committed to a multicultural approach will all reflect the values and belief systems of a diverse, multicultural community.

Another aspect of creating a classroom that authentically reflects a community is the involvement of parents and family members. Throughout this book there are suggestions about how to bring people who are important in the lives of your students into the educational process. Be as creative as possible in finding ways to integrate the children's home and school lives by being inclusive of the families' cultures and experiences.

In this chapter, six elements of the learning environment for young children are discussed: language arts, social studies, blocks, dramatic play, music and games, and cooking. While science and mathematics are not formally addressed, there are many concepts from each of these subject areas included, and activities are integrated into descriptions of other aspects of the learning environment and the unit in Chapter 6. For example, cooking activities alone are filled with science and math concepts: measuring; adding ingredients; studying how individual ingredients change as they are mixed together; counting the number of stirrings it takes to mix flour into cake batter; comparing how foods taste and feel before and after they are cooked. By asking what happens to each of the individual ingredients as they are mixed with others while making cookies, for example, you are encouraging the children to create a hypothesis and to become curious about changes in foods. Your task is to highlight those pieces of an activity that pertain to science or to math and then to build on them by creating related activities.

LANGUAGE ARTS

Books and language-experience activities frequently take up a large part of the child's day in preschool. Through activities like group discussions, each child has the opportunity to go beyond the boundaries of his or her own environment and to increase her or his understanding of and sensitivity to other people's lives. For example, in Katherine Paterson's book *The Tale of the Mandarin Ducks*, children see people taking risks to do what is right even though their actions may put them in danger. *Black Is Brown Is Tan*, by Arnold Adoff, gives a child who is growing up in a family of one racial heritage a sense of the experience of bi- or multiracial children. It also confirms for bi- and multiracial children that their lives are important and valued. Including families of a variety of configurations in language-arts activities allows children to learn about the life experiences of others. (For all of the recommended children's books, publication information and annotations are given in Appendix B.)

Guidelines

Using multicultural guidelines in choosing books and activities is basic to a multicultural program. The following is a beginning list of guidelines for choosing books and other materials for language arts (such as magazines, books with tapes, tapes of stories and folk tales, books of poems, or stories to be told to children). They are meant as suggestions rather than hard and fast rules. You will probably add other guidelines as you increase your own sensitivity to cultural diversity.

- How are differences in skin colors, lifestyles, or value systems treated? Are characters with skin colors, value systems, or lifestyles other than White and middle class presented in a positive light?
  - Are the characters presented in a way that encourages children of

diverse backgrounds to identify with them and care about them?
   • Are children portrayed as working together, each bringing her or his special skills and qualities to a problem?
   • Look at the street scenes, the playground and classroom scenes: How different are the children from one another? Could most children identify with the pictures?
   • Look at the roles of the characters: Are interests and abilities stereotyped according to the color or gender of each person?
   • How do authority figures interact with children? Is there respect on the part of each group?
   • How do children reading the books see adults of color in the books? What roles do adults of color play?
   • What is the vocabulary of the book? Look carefully at the use of words such as *black* and *white.* Is *black* associated with negative things or *white* with positive experiences even if race is not being talked about? Examine the use of dialect to see if it is authentic and necessary to the story or a stereotypic gimmick.
   • Are picture books describing historical situations written from a White

viewpoint? Are Native Americans presented as subhuman or one-dimensional? Do the people of various races (for example, all of the Asians) look alike? Is history skewed so that everything is presented from the Western European perspective?

- Are differences presented as odd or other than normal? Is the person in the picture who is different being mocked or made fun of?
- Are children seen as strong characters? Are boys presented as "doers" and girls as "observers," or are risk takers of both genders presented? Are children empowered problem-solvers or following in their parents' footsteps?
- Do the books help children make sense of what they are seeing or experiencing, for example, death, divorce, and other kinds of change?
- If a book was published more than ten years ago, does it reflect current sensitivities? For example, in several of the books written by Ingri and Edgar D'Aulaire, such as *Pocahontas* (New York: Doubleday, 1949) and *George Washington* (New York: Doubleday, 1936), the Black people are treated as less-than-human oddities and the Native Americans as cartoon-like dancing animals.

Clearly, if you applied all of these guidelines to the assessment of each book or other language-arts material, you would have to dispose of the majority of your collection. There are, however, a couple of less drastic ways to deal with this problem. First, you can focus on removing particularly offensive materials from the classroom. Books such as Helen Bannerman's *Little Black Sambo* (Cutchogue, NY: Buccaneer Books, 1983), which was originally published in 1899 and has remained in print ever since, rely so heavily on racial stereotypes, such as the idea of Black people's wearing very colorful clothes, that it is impossible to separate what might be true from what is stereotype. Because most young children are not developmentally able to distinguish between what is true and what is not true (that is, between reality and fantasy), they take the stereotyped misinformation as fact.

Second, because very few books fall into the "all good" or "all bad" categories, you can talk to children about the books that are being read, ask them what they think about the stories, and help them think about what they are seeing. Ezra Jack Keats' *The Snowy Day*, for example, has received a good deal of criticism for its presentation of the Black mother. She is described as big and warm, and she looks like the stereotype that many White cultures perpetuate of Black mothers. On the other hand, she *is* warm and nurturing, providing love and a stable place to come back to after an enjoyable outing. For many children (and adults) there could be nothing better. You might ask the African American children in the class if their mothers look like the one in the picture. Children from other racial and cultural backgrounds might also have mothers who look like *The Snowy Day* mother. You could ask how their mothers are the same and how they are different from this one. In a class that does not include Black children, one can ask if the mother in the story looks like the mother in another book about a Black family or like any of the children's mothers in size, shape, and behavior, even if not in color. In this way the children are encouraged to think about what they are seeing rather than simply taking the pictures as representative of all African American women.

Bread and Jam for Frances and *Bedtime for Frances*, two of the Frances books written by Russell Hoban, are stories about a badger family. They are much too good to pass up, even though the parents are portrayed in traditional gender roles. The depiction of Frances authentically reflects the ways that many 3- and 4-year-olds think, complete with nonsensical rhymes about ordinary experiences like eating breakfast and skipping rope. Again, when reading the Frances books, you can simply remark to the children that Frances' mother works at home and her father goes out to work; lots of families do it differently.

You can also use books to introduce hard-to-talk-about subjects to children. Jeanette Winter's *Follow the Drinking Gourd* is the story of a family's using the Underground Railroad as it escapes from slavery. *Our Teacher's in a Wheelchair*, by Mary Ellen Powers, tells about a kindergarten teacher who uses a wheelchair as he spends his days with the children. *We Are All in the Dumps with Jack and Guy*, by Maurice Sendak, is the story of homeless children and how they survive. For sophisticated 4-year-olds and older children, particularly those who live in cities and see people living on the streets, the book offers some sense of hope and caring and of family other than as we usually think of it. In many classrooms today there are children who are homeless, or who have been, and the book presents this life as an understandable reality.

The Use of Language

In the United States, great importance is placed on how "articulate" one is, on the level of English one speaks (that is, its closeness to "standard" English), and on the way one expresses oneself. A large measure of racism, classism, and sexism are built into our vocabulary, just as they are built into all other areas of our lives. Racism, as well as sexism and classism, carry over into the language in which children's books are written. Almost 30 years ago Charlamae Rollins (1967) discussed the use of dialect in books for children. She observed that it is neither correct nor fair to portray Black people as always speaking in dialect and maintained that for the author to create a "false idiom" or to make up a dialect using words such as "dat" and "dem" is racist. She also pointed out, however, that we each speak in a dialect and that to write in the dialect that is our own gives the reader a better sense of the characters in the story. She urged that "just as stereotyped portrayal of the Negro must be replaced by a sensitive, accurate portrayal, so the caricature of his language should be replaced by accurate, understandable use of the vernacular" (p. xv). Since we don't always know if the dialect used in a specific book is authentic (as opposed to stereotypic), the safest solution is to use books written in Black English by Black authors. While children's books that depict Black experiences in America have moved a long way toward Rollins' goals of sensitive and accurate portrayal, we still have much farther to go to be bias-free. And we can never be too careful about the books we give children to read.

In creating a strong collection of language-arts materials, be sure to include books that are written either for children who don't speak English or who speak English as their second language. With the number of immigrants in the United States rising rapidly, you can no longer assume that all of your students will speak English nor can you afford to use only books and materials written in English. *Regardless of the cultural make-up of the class*, including bilingual materials or simple materials written completely in languages other than English helps children learn new languages and see other ways of expressing themselves.

Diversity of Materials

Supplying a variety of language-arts materials and experiences is necessary to the multicultural approach to a curriculum. Children can learn about cultures other than their own by simply looking at pictures from ethnic magazines such as *Essence, Hispanic, Ebony, ¡HOLA!, Jet, News from Native California, Japan Pictorial, China Today,* and *Contenido.* (You need to beware, however, of journals like *National Geographic Magazine* that frequently present people of color as strange or exotic, so different from anyone a child growing up in the United States has any familiarity with that the people and their customs seem weird and bizarre.) Folk tales provide an enormous amount of insight into a group's cultural heritage, although you have to be extremely careful in choosing folk-tale collections. Too often fairy tales, folk tales, and fables reinforce stereotypes of the people about whom they are written. Poems from various cultures also give children a sense of how different people use language. The greater the variety of listening and preliteracy experiences children have, the more likely they are to grow to cherish reading, to affirm differences in others, and be willing to share their own stories.

A Final Note About Language Arts

My intention here is to provide some guidelines and thoughts about creating a multicultural approach to language arts, *not* to describe a preliteracy program for young children. I do, however, want to call attention to one element of the ongoing dialogue in the field of teaching reading. It pertains directly to the purpose of *Diversity in the Classroom* and reminds us that we constantly have to examine the ways we teach to see if they affect one group of children differently than others.

The tension surrounding the debate about the process-oriented approach (Whole Language) versus the skills-oriented approach is a difficult one to address briefly. Those of us who are progressive, middle- and upper-middle-class educators who believe strongly in the tenets and practices of open education would probably design a prereading program following a Whole Language approach.

> The basic belief in Whole Language is that students must actively engage in reading and writing experiences instead of working on exercises or developing "make believe" language or reading skills. Students assimilate knowledge of language when they immerse themselves in meaningful language experiences. (Saracho, 1993, p. 44)

I have often heard myself speak scornfully about teachers who use ditto sheets or skills workbooks. Before reading an article by Lisa Delpit (1988), I had never consciously thought of the ramifications of one of the middle-class privileges I have been given: being of a class and culture in which the grammatical rules that undergird the process-oriented approach are part of my daily experience. Not only was I taught the rules of "standard" English from a very early age, I was corrected any time I got confused. (If, as an elementary school child, for example, I had said, "I did real good on my test," I would not only have been reminded that I had made a mistake, but I would also have been told the rule: that *real* and *good* are adjectives and I needed the adverbs *really* and *well.* I would have corrected myself to "I did really well" without much effort.) In many ways the Whole Language approach assumes, or is at least strengthened by, a home life in which reading and writing are valued and a rich variety of reading materials exists that model "standard" English.

It is important to point out that the proponents of the two approaches often divide along racial and socioeconomic lines. Delpit (1988) believes that, when you are teaching poor White children and children of color, you have a responsibility to give them the rules of "standard" English explicitly, rather than assuming that they will get them by osmosis if they are immersed in mainstream culture and "standard" English.

> Although the problem is not necessarily inherent in the method, in some instances adherents of the process approaches to writing create situations in which students ultimately find themselves held accountable for knowing a set of rules about which no one has ever directly informed them. Teachers do students no service to suggest, even implicitly, that "product" is not important. In this country, students will be judged on their product regardless of the process they utilized to achieve it. And that product, based as it

is on the specific codes of a particular culture, is more readily produced
when the directives of how to produce it are made explicit. (p. 287)

I obviously believe that a rich and diverse selection of materials and varied
opportunities for experiential learning are vital to a good language-arts reading program. However, I also believe that, for many children, direct teaching of skills is necessary in addition.

The essence of my concern is this: Although providing an extremely
rich and diverse language-arts curriculum, you might be adding to the
inequities experienced by some children by not explicitly giving them the
language rules necessary for success in the dominant culture, a culture that
not only is not theirs but also is, in fact, hostile to them. The task is to reassess
what each of your students needs to be able to be successful in mainstream
America and then to provide opportunities for each to gain those skills without giving up her or his own culture.

SOCIAL STUDIES

In addition to meeting the caretaking needs of the parents, one of the chief
purposes of putting young children in a group situation such as a nursery
school, a day-care center, or a preschool is to help them learn to be social
beings; developing social skills is a major component in many young children's
days. Social studies is the part of a preschool curriculum that concentrates
on helping children develop human-relations skills. It cannot be confined
to one specific learning area or set time in a school day; social education
goes on all the time in the classroom. Children are constantly trying to figure themselves out, both personally and in relation to other people and to
objects in their environment.

Social studies is inherently multicultural. It concerns itself with preparing children to enter into diverse inter-group relations, as well as with giving them skills and knowledge needed to function in an increasingly changing world. Part of the rationale for a social-studies curriculum is to help
children increase their understanding and acceptance of attitudes, values,
and lifestyles that are unfamiliar to them.

In developing a social-studies curriculum for young children, it is important to remember that they are primarily concerned with themselves and
their immediate surroundings. While a social-studies curriculum for older
children often examines communities far away and considers how other cultures deal with their environments, teachers who work with young children
need to create atmospheres in which children can learn about themselves
and each other as social beings and in which ongoing multicultural experi-

ences are provided. In a heterogeneous class, this multicultural experience will include immediate contact with children of other backgrounds. In a monocultural setting, regardless of the culture represented, it is especially important that the teacher provide a multicultural environment through thoughtful selection of curriculum materials and learning activities that reflect our society. In this way, younger children will be better prepared for diverse experiences as they grow older.

When selecting curriculum materials, you should guard against racial, ethnic, and sex-role stereotypes, as well as against ethnocentricity. Too often the world is presented from a White, middle-class American point of view; for example, stories may describe families as consisting of mother, father, and two children, and other family configurations are implicitly seen as less than adequate. The damage of having your own childhood experience identified as not whole is far-reaching. I vividly remember being told in elementary school that my mother couldn't be a class parent because, since my father was dead, we weren't a "real" family.

Cultural differences such as styles of dress, foods, or ways of doing things are too often presented as foreign, quaint, exotic, or plain wrong. Presenting material in this manner encourages intolerance rather than openness in children. (In many ways, the curriculum unit presented in Chapter 6 is one in social studies. For specifics about how to apply social-studies theory and multicultural education to everyday teaching, refer back to Chapter 6.)

UNIT BLOCKS

Building with unit blocks is frequently a large part of the early childhood curriculum. Developed by Caroline Pratt in the early 1900s, unit blocks are a medium through which children can recreate their own experiences. Pratt saw blocks as the most basic learning tool in a curriculum; they are still used as one of the essential play materials in the school she founded in New York City (Hirsch, 1974). Unit blocks have no color and no guiding design, so children control what they build and how. Children are in charge, not the materials. Through working with blocks, children see that they can change the world—blocks are transformational materials. Further,

> building with blocks utilizes skills from all the cognitive domains like math (number and pattern), science (balance and gravity), social studies (copying architectural monuments), art (form and design), and physical (large and small muscle utilization). Playing with blocks is mainly a social event with roles being played out with blocks as the medium. Both building and playing are important skills in the block center, and the teacher's job is to encourage each child to utilize both aspects. (Stritzel, 1995, p. 47)

Playing with blocks reinforces the goals of multicultural education by allowing for a variety of learning styles, by encouraging cooperative play, and by providing opportunities for children to work interdependently. Unit blocks can be used effectively as a primary learning tool with children from $1\frac{1}{2}$ to 8 or 9 years old. With very young children (2 and younger), a few blocks and simple shapes are most useful (Hirsch, 1974, p. 105).

Children's building increases in complexity as the children become less egocentric. For older children, working with blocks is a good way to begin acquiring map-making skills. Lucy Sprague Mitchell's *Young Geographers* (1971) describes a process through which children can begin to make sense of their environment by building what it looks like to them. I know of one classroom of 6- to 8-year-olds in New York City in which the children built a replica of what Manhattan looks like from the street down. (At the top of the construction was the street level, then the subway, then the sewer system.) Because we live in a country that has been called geographically illiterate, we need to help children understand the relationships between themselves and their environment. Using *Young Geographers* as a resource when setting up block play provides us with ways to integrate geography, social studies, and science that encourage children to be explorers themselves, rather than simply reading about others' explorations.

Block-corner accessories must reflect a multicultural perspective. In both homogeneous and heterogeneous classrooms, the people block accessories can mirror a multicultural community so that children are helped to develop a culturally diverse frame of reference. Community helpers and family members should be multiracial and non-stereotypic in terms of race or sex roles. As suggested in Chapter 6, if you are unable to purchase a wide selection of people block accessories, make your own using pictures of the children's families or magazine pictures mounted and laminated on blocks of wood.

Block building has myriad possibilities, but, if you are not comfortable with the blocks, the children probably will not be either. To become better acquainted with blocks, spend some time building with them. You also might photograph children working together in the block corner, display photographs of their buildings, and make a book of the photograph collection for the reading or library area. The more you enjoy and appreciate building, the better the children will feel about devoting their energies to blocks and the more they will learn.

The hardest aspect of using blocks in the classroom is that, unfortunately, the block corner is *still* seen as the boys' domain; girls often are not welcome there. You can help to counter this by encouraging girls to work with blocks. The block area might be placed next to the housekeeping or dramatic-play area. Boys and girls are then more likely to explore both areas by combining their dramatic-play activity with block building.

Although it seems likely to me that there is a connection between girls' lack of experience with blocks and their later math deficiencies, I have been able to find no current research exploring this possibility. The lack of research on the effects of girls' being excluded from the block corner, intentionally or unintentionally, was confirmed for me by Harriet Cuffaro (personal communication, May 15, 1995), who has dedicated much of her professional research to block play. (See Cuffaro, 1995.) She and I both find this lack of research disturbing and connect it to the myth that sexism is a thing of the past and we no longer need to be concerned.

I point out this situation as an example of the subtle ways that sexism works. Many people seem to feel that sexism as it pertains to young girls is not worth examining. Shockingly, by 1991, "...[n]ational studies on the shortchanging of girls in education [have] been conducted at the high school and college levels, but...no such work [has] been undertaken at the most formative stages of a child's upbringing, the elementary school years" (Trowbridge, 1995, p. 1). However, as you can see in the relevant discussions in Chapter 3 and in the Epilogue, there are many educators who are deeply concerned. The message for you, as teachers, is to pay close attention to the ways in which girls and boys use the classroom. If you see areas that are either boy- or girl-dominated, think about ways to involve children of the other gender as well. While the effects of gender bias in the block area are currently undocumented, we cannot afford to ignore our hunches.

DRAMATIC PLAY

Dramatic play is one of the most important aspects of the young child's curriculum, and it has enormous potential in a multicultural classroom. As
explained in Chapter 2, through dramatic play children are able to try on
many roles and behaviors to see how they fit.

In order for children to use the dramatic-play area most advantageous-
ly, the roles available within the area should not be limited by ethnocentricity
or sex-role stereotypes. No one cultural group should be over-represented
either in the pictures on the walls or in the general atmosphere of the area.
In many classrooms the dramatic-play area is basically a kitchen/eating area
and a bedroom. If there is enough space, the teacher can add a living room
so that children can sit down and talk to one another, either as they see
grown-ups do at home or as they would like to see grown-ups do. Instead of
lace, pastel colors, and flowery prints, canvas curtains and striped bedspreads
can be used in the bedroom to avoid a stereotypically feminine atmosphere.
A comfortable lounge chair and a rocking chair as well as a table and chairs
for use at mealtime might be included. It is also good to change the area
around from time to time so that it represents styles of living in various cultures. For example, a mat might be put on the floor to use as a bed or a ham-
mock might be strung to help children understand that different people
have various furniture for sleeping.

When the clothes in the dramatic-play area are neatly stored and well
organized, the children know where to find things as well as where to put
things back when they are finished with them. Including clothes from several cultures, such as a kimono and a dashiki, gives children the additional
opportunity of learning the proper names for these garments as well as allowing them to experience wearing clothes from a variety of cultures. The children need work clothes as well as fancy clothes, everyday shoes as well as
dressy ones. You can also provide all sorts of women's and men's clothes,
not just suits or jackets worn by white-collar workers. For example, a work shirt
makes a great construction worker's uniform. It is also a good idea to have
overalls or painter's pants, using sizes that are not too big or cutting the
clothes down to size so they won't fall off the children or trip them. Every
kind of hat imaginable can go into the dramatic-play area: a miner's hat, a
baseball cap, scarves, turbans. In addition to clothes, children love to play with
pieces of cloth; they can make them into capes, robes, sashes, dresses, or
tablecloths. A few pieces of cloth can add many new dimensions to the clothes
collection.

In her book *Non-Sexist Education for Young Children*, Barbara Sprung
(1975) reported that having more briefcases and fewer purses in the dramatic-play area encouraged boys and girls to do more dramatic play about

going to work. (While this research is 20 years old, I believe it is still valid.) In addition to briefcases, you can supply other work props such as lunch boxes, tool belts, backpacks, or big canvas bags that can be used as mail-carrier pouches, tool bags, or grocery bags. Additionally, you can include clothes that are appropriate for older people, as well as clothes for parents and for children. Anything is possible in dramatic play, so children's imaginations should be stimulated rather than limited by the props available for their use.

Since dolls are "one of the first abstract symbols used by children to replace the self as an object of play" (Sprung, 1975, p. 30), they are extremely valuable in helping a child develop a strong self-concept. Providing a wide selection of multiracial dolls in the dramatic-play area is therefore critical. Both boys and girls need dolls that look like them, as well as dolls that look like other children in the community. In an all-White class a multiracial selection of dolls encourages children to engage in hypothetical interactions with people of color. Through observing this play, you will be able to gain information about how the children perceive other racial groups. In a heterogeneous class the dolls become a reflection of the class community. When selecting dolls, avoid those that represent children of color as having exactly the same features as the White ones and choose those that authentically represent the facial characteristics of various people of color.

The dramatic-play area is one of the most crucial in the classroom. For some children it represents a microcosm, a space in which they can be in control as they see adults in control outside the dramatic-play area. For other children it is an opportunity to move from the all-too-real world to one in which life is not so hard. In order to be inviting to all children, regardless of race or gender, the dramatic play area needs to have items in it that are culturally diverse.

MUSIC AND GAMES

Taking a multicultural approach to music and games is not only easy but also is a great deal of fun. All it takes is a commitment to more careful selection of materials, keeping in mind the goal of overall multiculturalism in the classroom. It is important to talk to the children about the music they listen to and sing as well as about the games they play, so that they are aware that different cultural groups or "kinds of people" listen to various kinds of music and play games. Through culturally diverse music and games, the children are learning about other people's lives. It is important to remember, however, that music and games are not the culture itself but rather a visible reflection of values and belief systems. Often, when we talk about multicultural education, we think about tangible things rather than looking at the values and beliefs beneath the surface. For example, the extent of interaction and involvement of the choir and the congregation in many African American Protestant churches reflects the belief that being a part of the religious experience brings you closer to God. Call and response is valued as participation in worship. While other churches, specifically some predominantly White denominations, value participation too, how that interaction takes place is different. The expression of feeling and experience is more active and vocal in one than in the other. Each group's church service mirrors the values of the respective culture.

Music

There is a lot of music available for children that reflects the cultures from which it stems; for example, folk songs have been recorded from almost every ethnic group in this country. So that children can get a sense of music from other countries as well, simple songs sung in languages other than English should be included in the collection of tapes in the classroom.

It is good to have a listening area in the classroom with tapes, cassette players, and two or three sets of earphones. Some older children may be able to work with the equipment themselves; otherwise the teacher must be responsible for changing records or tapes. If there is enough space, the listening area can be made cozy with a pillow or two and can be partitioned off so that it is somewhat removed from the rest of the classroom. If the teacher values this area and transmits that message to the children by the way the area is arranged, the children will see the listening area as an integral part of their work, not just somewhere to go when the "real" work is finished. Children will also enjoy time in the day for singing and listening to music in a large group. Most young children like to sing with their friends, so it does not take too much encouragement to produce a chorus.

Another way to enjoy music is to make it. Children can create their own musical instruments, using instruments from other cultures as models. For example, they can make instruments that resemble maracas by putting dried pumpkin seeds in paper cups, covering the tops of the cups with pieces of paper, and taping the papers to the sides of the cups. Before the children make maracas, you can show them real ones and talk about how some children use maracas to make music. You could also read a book to the children about Spanish-speaking children making music. (See Appendix B.) There are lots of musical instruments the children can make for very little money, and other instruments, such as castanets or triangles, are available commercially at relatively low cost. With some guidance from you, children can spend many hours exploring cultural diversity through music.

Games

Playing games is a universal activity for children. Across cultures, children today play games that were played hundreds and, in some cases, thousands of years ago. Each successive generation of children believes it has created the games. Moreover, children all over the world play many of the same games with only minor changes from culture to culture. (Opie & Opie, 1969.)

Applying a multicultural approach to the games played in a classroom requires much the same kind of ingenuity necessary for using culturally diverse music in the curriculum. Teachers can do two things: call on the ethnic resources within the school community, and do research to find age-appropriate games played by children of various cultural heritages. In a heterogeneous classroom the children themselves are sources for games played in their cultures. The sharing of games will not only be a source of enjoyment but also a way to give the children a better understanding of their friends' ethnic heritages.

COOKING

Cooking is one of the most important of all activities in a preschool curriculum because it supports growth in four developmental areas: emotional, social, intellectual, and physical. Emotionally, cooking and eating what has been cooked provide a shared classroom experience. Because working together is basic to cooking activities, children acquire social skills while they are making something to eat. Measuring, weighing, pouring, and following a recipe help children acquire concepts, skills, and knowledge related to several curriculum areas, specifically mathematics, science, social studies, and language arts. Children's physical development is promoted as they practice fine motor skills required for cutting, peeling, and slicing. Eye–hand coordination and sensory discrimination skills are also used by children as they cook.

A multicultural approach to cooking has two goals: first, to encourage children to experiment with food other than that with which they are familiar and, second, to give young children a general notion of the connections between cultural heritage and the process of preparing, cooking, and eating a meal. The first goal can be met by providing children with diverse eating experiences. You can reach the second goal by presenting a variety of ways of preparing, cooking, and eating food. For example, a teacher might decide to do a short unit on breads from various cultures. As children make tortillas, cornbread, pita bread, matzos, and whole wheat bread, they are able to compare the processes and can talk about the ways in which the processes are the same and the ways in which they are different. Without giving children stereotypic information about cultures and foods—Chinese people eat rice, Latinos eat beans, White people eat cheeseburgers—you can help children see basic connections between cooking and cultural heritage. (This unit is more appropriate for 4- and 5-year-olds than for 3-year-olds.) Children can understand that different groups of people may grow the same vegetables in their gardens—corn, for example—and use them to make various foods that are basic to their daily lives—tortillas, cornbread, polenta, cornmeal mush, spoon-bread.

Habitat as well as culture, of course, greatly influences what food is grown and how it is prepared and served. While it would not be helpful to give young children an abundance of specific information about where various foods are grown or why some cultures cook with different spices than others, it is possible to help children understand basic concepts about the relation of food to habitat and culture. The teacher can illustrate the influence of habitat on what people grow and eat by using developmentally appropriate examples, such as people who live by the sea and eat fish or people who have vegetable gardens and eat the corn, beans, and tomatoes they grow. Through cooking activities children gain concrete experience of the concept that there are some things all groups of people do but the ways in which they are done vary from group to group.

As suggested in the unit in Chapter 6, the recipes used can be saved to make a cookbook for the children. One might begin with recipes that include ingredients the children like to eat, such as African chicken stew with peanuts or quesadillas (tortillas with cheese). Recipes and cooking activities should be fairly simple. It is helpful to write the directions clearly on a recipe chart, including pictures of ingredients and symbols for measurements, so that children who are beginning to learn to read can start matching pictures and words. Depending on the facilities available, children can prepare a cold snack or an entire hot meal.

The children's families are one of the best sources for recipes. Some children may have recipes that have been in their families for a long time. On the other hand, some families may not have resources for planned meals that include the use of recipes; for many people eating is an issue of survival or a time for "grazing" rather than a sharing, family time. Thus it is important to be conscious of the role food plays in individual children's lives. Other ways of finding out what people from various cultures eat are to look in an encyclopedia or in magazines from various ethnic groups, to read stories about different cultures, and to look in cookbooks that focus on particular ethnic groups.

Cooking with children provides many opportunities to bring a multicultural perspective to the curriculum. It offers children the opportunity to begin to broaden their taste in foods by eating dishes from a variety of ethnic cuisines. Children can also begin to make the connections between food and cultural heritage by cooking with the parents of others in the classroom.

EVALUATING THE CLASSROOM ENVIRONMENT

As you begin to develop a multicultural classroom environment you will want to evaluate progress in each of the areas discussed in this chapter. The Multicultural Classroom Environment Checklist which follows provides specific questions to help you rate your progress in each area. By using the checklist, you will focus on individual aspects of the classroom environment and curriculum, highlighting areas that need improvement. You are encouraged to rate the classroom as it is currently, not as you would like it to be.

Multicultural Classroom Environment Checklist

OVERALL ENVIRONMENT

1. In general is the classroom hospitable?
   Are the walls painted a pleasing color?
   　　　Yes __　No __
   Is the room clean and tidy?
   　　　Yes __　No __
   Are there touches of softness—for example, a rug and pillows in the book area, a rug in the dramatic-play area?
   　　　Yes __　No __
   Are all of the work areas clearly identified so that the children can choose on their own where they would like to be?
   　　　Yes __　No __

2. What is hanging on the walls?
   If there is work done by children, does it all look alike? For example, are there bunnies or other animals that you have cut out and the children colored or is the art *genuinely* done by the children?
   　　　Yes __　No __
   If no, how will you change the art experiences to allow for greater creativity?
   Are the pictures of people hanging on walls or bulletin boards representative of a multicultural community?
   　　　Yes __　No __
   If no, what pictures will you add?
   Even if pictures *do* represent a diverse population, are they stereotypic in any way? For example, is there an alphabet chart that uses "Indian" to symbolize the letter "I" or a calendar that features little girls wearing dresses watching little boys involved in activities? Are there Hawaiians in grass skirts or people from South America sparsely clothed and with spears and painted faces?
   　　　Yes __　No __

3. Are all of the pictures for children and the art hung *at children's eye-level?*
   Yes __ No __

4. Are parents and/or family members involved in creating a hospitable classroom environment?
   Yes __ No __
   If yes, how do you include them? How might you make them feel
   even more a part of their children's school lives?

LANGUAGE ARTS

1. Does the classroom have a wide variety of age-appropriate and cul-
   turally diverse books and language-arts materials?
   Yes __ No __
   What are the strengths of the collection in general?
   Where are there gaps?

2. Are there stories about a variety of people from each of the follow-
   ing groups in the book corner?
   _____ Native American cultures
   _____ Asian American cultures
   _____ Black cultures
   _____ White ethnic cultures
   _____ Spanish-speaking cultures
   _____ biracial or multiracial people
   _____ family configurations, including biracial and multiracial fam-
   ilies and gay and lesbian families

3. Are there any books that speak of people of diverse cultures in
   stereotypic or derogatory terms (for example, describing Latinos as
   "lazy" or Japanese as always taking photographs)?
   Yes __ No __
   If yes, what are they? What new titles can you replace them with?

SOCIAL STUDIES

1. Does the curriculum as a whole help the children increase their
   understanding and acceptance of attitudes, values, and lifestyles that
   are unfamiliar to them?
   Yes __ No __
   If yes, how?
   If no, what will you do to change your current curriculum so that it
   reflects a diversity of values?

2. Are materials and games racially or sex-role stereotypic—for example, Black people shooting dice or boys playing war games? Are women depicted only as caregivers while men do lots of exciting jobs?

    Yes __ No __

    If yes, what will you weed from your current collection?
    What materials and games can you add that decrease stereotypes?

BLOCKS

1. Are the accessories in the block area representative of various cultural groups and family configurations?

    Yes __ No __

    List them below to be sure that no major cultural group or family configuration is missing.

2. Are the people block accessories stereotypic in terms of sex roles?

    Yes __ No __

    If yes, how will you change them?

DRAMATIC PLAY

1. Is there a wide variety of clothes, including garments from various cultural groups, in the dramatic-play area?

    Yes __ No __

    If yes, what are they?
    If no, what do you need to add?

2. Are the pictures on the walls and the props in the dramatic-play area representative of a diversity of cultures?

    Yes __ No __

    If yes, what is included?
    If no, what do you need to add?

3. Are the dolls in the dramatic-play area representative of a broad variety of racial groups?

    Yes __ No __

    If no, what do you need to add?

4. Are the dolls of color just White dolls whose skin color has been changed?

    Yes __ No __

    If so, which ones need replacing?

MUSIC AND GAMES

1. Do the music experiences in the curriculum reinforce the children's affirmation of cultural diversity?

    Yes __ No __

    If so, how?

2. Are finger plays, games, and songs from various cultural groups used in the classroom?

    Yes __ No __

3. Are there many varieties of musical instruments, including ones made by children, in the classroom?

    Yes __ No __

COOKING

1. Do the cooking experiences in the classroom encourage the children to experiment with foods other than those with which they are familiar?

    Yes __ No __

2. Are the cooking experiences designed to give young children a general notion of the connections between cultural heritage and the process of preparing, cooking, and eating food?

    Yes __ No __

    If so, how?

    If not, what can you do differently to help children make those connections?

Epilogue

Moving Forward

I find, as I complete the revision of this book, that there are many paths I want to take next, many thoughts and challenges I am left with and want to mention here—none with answers, none completely researched. Over and over I find myself writing, "I would be irresponsible not to mention...." Moving forward requires, for each of us, that we look deeper into ourselves and with a panoramic eye at the world.

UNFINISHED WORK

There are three issues that are pressing on me, not to be left in my computer in the file called "Odds and Ends of Writing—Unused." My hope is that each will motivate you, as it has me, to look more deeply into the intersections of race, gender, and early childhood education. I hope they will move you to read more, think more, have conversations with different people, or have different conversations with the people you usually talk with. The first is about what is happening to young girls and how we as educators must change the school experience for them so that they can survive as whole human beings. The second and third are about the ways, which some find extremely subtle, in which institutional racism does its pernicious work in child development and early childhood education: through the "marginalizing" (hooks, 1990) and the silencing of people of color (Delpit, 1988) so that we who are White may or may not listen, but, regardless, we do not *hear*.

Creating Environments in Which Girls Can Flourish

Recently much has been written about what is happening to girls in school, and the reports are overwhelmingly negative (see Brown & Gilligan, 1992; Gilligan, 1990; Orenstein, 1994; Pipher, 1994). Myra and David Sadker have been studying gender inequity in schools for more than 20 years. In *Failing at Fairness* (1994), they chronicle the myriad ways in which girls have a different school experience from boys and its effects on later life. Teachers report that their least-favorite students are aggressive girls. In school classrooms, boys are three times more likely to be praised than girls and eight times more likely to call out answers than girls.

> Whether male comments are insightful or irrelevant, teachers respond to them. However, when girls call out, there is a fascinating occurrence: Suddenly the teacher remembers the rule about raising your hand before you talk. And then the girl, who is usually not as assertive as the male students, is deftly and swiftly put back in her place.... It occurs several times a day during each school week for twelve years, and even longer if Kimberly goes on to college, and, most insidious of all, it happens subliminally. This microinequity eventually has a powerful cumulative effect. (pp. 43–44)

One of the studies discussed by the Sadkers was conducted by the American Association of University Women in 1990 and titled "How Schools Shortchange Girls." It found that girls' self-esteem, both as human beings and as students, changes far more dramatically in middle childhood than boys' does. For example, in elementary school 60% of girls report that they are happy about themselves; by the time they are in middle school it drops to 37% and still lower to 29% in high school. While the percentages for boys also changed, the results were not so extreme; 67% were happy about themselves in elementary school and by high school 46% were—a 21-point difference for boys versus 31 points for girls. Teachers are generally unconscious of the ways in which their behaviors contribute to the inferior school experiences of girls. Yet this experience has an appalling effect on them. Girls' IQ test scores fall 13 points in adolescence, while boys' scores drop only 3 points.

There is an extremely interesting twist in the results of this research. When the variable of race was isolated, the AAUW study found that Hispanic girls' scores, like those of girls overall, decreased; in fact, their drop was the sharpest, from 68% of them reporting in elementary school that they "always felt happy about themselves" (p. 79) to only 30% in high school. However, African American girls' sense of self grew more positive as they got older: "In elementary school, 59% of African-American girls considered themselves 'important,' a percentage that climbed to a healthy 74% by high school" (p. 79). This finding supports what Gilligan (1990) describes in a study done at the Emma Willard

School. African American girls' self-esteem appears not to be nearly so vulnerable to their teachers' gender-based treatment as that of girls of other races. It seems that Black girls' self-esteem is predominantly influenced by their mothers' judgments, while teachers' behaviors more strongly affect other girls' senses of themselves. (This is *not* to minimize the impact of teachers' negative racial attitudes on African American girls' school performance.)

In another study described in *Failing at Fairness*, one done by Lyn Mikel Brown and Carol Gilligan (1992) and published in their book *Meeting at the Crossroads: Women's Psychology and Girls' Development*, it was found that

> girls learned to censor themselves. Younger children spoke in clear, strong, authentic voices. As they moved up in grade, their voices became modulated, softened, and sometimes obliterated. Lively and outspoken and able to express a range of feelings at seven and eight, they became more reticent as they grew older; they monitored themselves and one another with adult prescriptions for "good girl" behavior: "Be nice," "Talk quietly," "Be calm," "Cooperate." (p. 90)

Finally, and most disturbing to me, are the findings from a decade long study done by the Sadkers (1994) themselves in schools across the country. They asked children how they would feel if they woke up and found they were members of the other gender. The girls' responses ranged from being disappointed because they liked being girls to being happy because, if they were boys, they would be able to have the choices boys have. The boys' responses were startling:

> "If I were a girl, my friends would treat me like dirt."
> "My teachers would treat me like a little hairy pig-headed girl."
> "I would hide and never go out until after dark."
> "I would *kill* myself *right away* by setting myself on fire so no one knew."
> "No cat liked me. No dog. No animal in the world. I did not like myself."
>   (pp. 83–84)

The challenge for you as teachers is to be ever mindful of your behavior toward girls as compared to your treatment of boys. For example, do you praise girls for how they look and boys for what they do? The Sadkers tell us that "the one area where girls are recognized more than boys is appearance. Teachers compliment their outfits and hairstyles" (p. 55). In this unconscious way teachers reinforce the stereotype of what an "attractive" girl is.

It is also crucial to be conscious of the devaluing comments and behaviors you allow. Just as it is not all right for children to be mean to one another on the basis of race, as was discussed in Chapter 5, it is also unacceptable for them to indicate that girls are of less value than boys. Children's comments such as "What do you know? You're just a girl" or "You're not a real

boy. You're a sissy" reinforce the sentiment that femaleness is less highly valued than maleness. Because the messages we receive in childhood have life-
long effects, the positive image of girls you present to all the children in
your class, the non-gender-biased information you give, and the fair expectations you have of all children will reinforce healthy development.

Resisting Marginalization

In the preface to *Feminist Theory: From Margin to Center*, bell hooks (1984)
writes about the different views of "the whole" that those who live in the margin have as opposed to those with privilege who live in "the center." While
she is speaking specifically about feminist theory, I believe that her words
apply equally to our concerns as educators.

> To be in the margin is to be part of the whole but outside the main body. As
> black Americans living in a small Kentucky town, the railroad tracks were a
> daily reminder of our marginality.... We looked both from the outside in and
> from the inside out. We focused our attention on the center as well as on the
> margin. (p. ix)

> Much...theory emerges from privileged [people] who live at the center,
> whose perspectives on reality rarely include knowledge and awareness of the
> lives of [those] who live in the margin. As a consequence [the] theory lacks
> wholeness, lacks the broad analysis that could encompass a variety of human
> experiences. (p. x)

I write about living in the margin because I believe that in the fields of
early childhood education and child development there is a danger of continuing to identify as "normal" the experiences of the White middle class and
to continue to relegate families/children who are "other" to the margin. Historically, early childhood education fell into this trap because most of developmental theory that forms the basis of our field was based on research by
and about White middle-class people. In an attempt to change the perception
of early childhood education as "women's work" to that of a legitimate field
of study, many theorists and practitioners talked about "the preschool child"
as if children were one entity, as if all normal children (as opposed to those
with special needs) go through the same developmental stages at roughly the
same ages and therefore have similar educational needs. Further, by prescribing a set of "developmentally appropriate" activities for "the child," it is
suggested that the societal, cultural, and familial contexts of children's lives
have little bearing on their needs and/or their development. Through this
process, the needs and experiences of children other than those who are part
of the mainstream middle class have been, and are still being, treated as
exceptions, moved from the center of the picture to the margin.

Recently I had a conversation with a child-development professional whose organization creates "multicultural" materials and guides teachers in using them. He said that there is one approach to teaching all children which, if done well, would meet every child's educational needs. Further, he said that there is no need to adjust this approach if one is teaching in a Latino neighborhood or an Asian one, a wealthy one or a poor one. For me, what he was saying is that those of us in what hooks calls "the center" have identified what all children need to learn. In addition, since this "one best way" is "child-centered" and is flexible enough to accommodate individual differences, all children will flourish. Sally Lubeck (1994) offers another perspective on what is involved in meeting the educational needs of children:

> If culture is, in fact, to be taken seriously, if parents and other community members have a say in how their children will be educated, then the very nature of programs and the ontological and epistemological assumptions on which they are based could differ. (p. 34)

What I believe Lubeck is saying is that we have an opportunity to create an educational system like none that has previously existed, one that genuinely serves the educational needs of children who come from vastly different cultures.

If this is to happen, those of us who have been and are at "the center" in early childhood education will have to put all of our theories, values and beliefs, and "best practices" on the table for reexamination. Moreover, we will have to open up the seating at the table and begin to share the power in decision-making, knowing that we might well disagree with the eventual outcomes. Only then will we be taking others' cultures seriously.

Instead, as hooks (1994) tells us,

> what we are witnessing today in our everyday life is not an eagerness on the part of neighbors and strangers to develop a world perspective but a return to narrow nationalism, isolationism, and xenophobia. These shifts are usually explained...as attempts to bring order to the chaos, to return to an (idealized) past. The notion of family evoked...is one in which sexist roles are upheld as stabilizing traditions.... This vision of family life is coupled with a notion of security that suggests we are always most safe with people of our same group, race, class, religion, and so on. (p. 28)

hooks is speaking to the movement in the United States to define as central the language, history, literature, and body of knowledge that represent upper-middle-class Western European culture and sensibilities. In 1987, Edward Hirsch published *Cultural Literacy: What Every American Needs to Know*. This is a sound-the-alarm book about how illiterate Americans are about

basic terms, facts, and concepts of our culture. He argues for a "return" to
a system of education that teaches all citizens an established vocabulary of
culture, so that we can talk together using the same system of cultural refer-
ents. (Simonson & Walker, 1988, p. ix)

Based on the enormous success of the first book, the next year Hirsch published a *Dictionary of Cultural Literacy,* a compendium of 5,000 words, concepts, quotations, names, and proverbs that "literate Americans" know. The
list was notable for the absence of references to anything other than White,
Western European culture. Michael Apple (1992) calls this "the politics of
official knowledge":

> It is during times of social upheaval that this relationship of education and
> power becomes most visible. Such a relationship was and continues to be
> made manifest in the struggles by women, people of color, and others to have
> their history and knowledge included in the curriculum. (p. 4)

Apple, like hooks, is talking about what and who are in the center and what
and who are kept in the margin.

Although policymakers and educators no longer talk about educating
those who are "culturally disadvantaged" or "culturally deprived" as they did
in the 1960s, embedded in the predominant theory and practices of early
childhood education is still the belief that "we"—European Americans—
know what is best for everyone's children. Intentionally or not, the guidelines
for developmentally appropriate practice created by the National Association for the Education of Young Children (Bredekamp, 1987), while more
subtle than the statements of 20 years ago, clearly establish who is central
and who is marginal

1. by defining dominant cultural practices as normal, positive, and uni-
    versally applicable; [and]
2. by claiming that it is incumbent upon those who are knowledgeable
    about "child development knowledge" to impart this knowledge to par-
    ents (thereby setting up a "we/they" relationship based on the privileged
    position of the professional). (Lubeck, 1994, pp. 20–21)

If we are to prepare children to live in our diverse nation and world,
none of us can afford to push aside ways of thinking and doing because they
are different from the ones with which we are most familiar and comfortable. The process of marginalizing diminishes us all. It allows those of us
who are European American to preserve the illusion that we are the only
holders of knowledge and renders us uneducated educators. Further, by
minimizing the essential knowledge and perspectives of those who are not
of the dominant culture of the educational policymakers (and whose input,

therefore, is excluded), we place the survival of children of color, and therefore our interdependent world, at risk.

Learning Not Just to Listen But to Hear

Some years back I was at my niece's wedding and heard a conversation about my older sister that proved illuminating. "Since you like to talk on the phone so much, why don't you get a CB [Citizens Band] radio in your car?" a friend had asked her. My sister's reply clarified an experience I had been having for years but didn't understand. "Oh, I only like to talk," she had said. "If I got a CB I would have to listen!" In fact, my experience is that she listens to *me* well, but I realized that in my immediate family the process of listening is not particularly valued. I know it to be essential in my work, so over the years I have deliberately learned to stop the never-ending conversations in my mind and attempt not only to listen but also to hear what people are saying.

Neither listening nor hearing is simple. Listening requires stopping the other voices in your head that are remembering that you forgot to turn off the oven before you left home, thinking about week-end plans, or (if you are like me) doing a running commentary on and preparing a response to the person to whom you are supposedly listening. Listening means closing out all of the outside noises and focusing on what the other person is saying. Hearing is related to listening, but it requires a greater commitment to communication. Really to hear others you have to be willing to open your mind and heart to them. You have to set aside your stereotypes, assumptions, and defenses to take in what the person is saying and feeling.

In many conversations there is an inherent power differential between the people who are speaking. In an interaction between teacher and child, the teacher has the power; in a discussion between a man and woman, the man is in the privileged position; in a conversation involving White people and people of color, the White people are the members of the culture of power. As was discussed in Chapter 3, having privilege (McIntosh, 1995) or being a member of the culture of power (Delpit, 1988) enables me to decide whether I am going to listen or hear or neither. As one of those in the culture of power, I also silence others without intending to or even being aware of it. In her article "The Silenced Dialogue: Power and Pedagogy in Educating Other People's Children," Delpit (1988) includes the extremely disturbing comments of an African American teacher describing her interactions with White teachers about the best ways to help children of color learn to read:

> "When you're talking to White people they still want it to be their way. You can try to talk to them and give them examples, but they're so headstrong, they think they know what's best for *everybody*, for *everybody's* children. They won't

listen, White folks are going to do what they want to do *anyway*.

"It's really hard. They just don't listen well. No, they listen, but they don't *hear*—you know how your mama used to say you listen to the radio, but you *hear* your mother? Well, they don't *hear* me.

"So I just try to shut them out so I can hold my temper. You can only beat your head against a brick wall for so long before you draw blood. If I try to stop arguing with them I can't help myself from getting angry. Then I end up walking around praying all day 'Please Lord, remove the bile I feel for these people so I can sleep tonight.' It's funny, but it can become a cancer, a sore.

"So, I shut them out. I go back to my own little cubby, my classroom, and I try to teach the way I know will work, no matter what those folk say. And when I get Black kids, I just try to undo the damage they did.

"I'm not going to let any man, woman, or child drive me crazy—White folks will try to do that if you let them. You just have to stop talking to them, that's what I do. I just keep smiling, but I won't talk to them." (pp. 280–281)

As Delpit says, these are not the sentiments of one isolated person who teaches in a particularly racist school. The feelings are representative of a vast number of people of color as they interact with White people on a daily basis.

The saddest element is that the individuals that the Black and Native American educators speak of...are seldom aware that the dialogue *has* been silenced. Most likely the White educators believe that their colleagues of color did, in the end, agree with their logic. After all, they stopped disagreeing, didn't they? (p. 281)

The African American teacher's comments haunt me. They sound so much like what I hear from people of color around the country, in schools, in colleges and universities, in corporations, in personal friendships. I struggled with whether or not to include the complete comments of the teacher. While I believe that they will confirm what people of color know, I fear that they will be bewildering, perhaps enraging, to many of us who are White. It is not often that we receive the gift of being privy to such personal feelings. My hope is that by including the comments in their entirety the impact will move us to *hear* as well as listen. And I hope that we will all move toward those conversations, no matter how painful, because we know that, if we don't, we will never be able to serve fully the children we care so deeply about.

FINALLY...

As always, we have choices. We can opt to bury our heads in the sand and rationalize about what is happening. We can also choose to reexamine how, what, why, and who we are teaching to see if we are empowering our students to live successfully in the multicultural world or if we are reinforcing the notion that

we only need to pay attention to people who are like us. I believe hooks (1994) is right as she speaks strongly to the necessity of retooling for the future:

> More than ever before in the recent history of this nation, educators are compelled to confront the biases that have shaped teaching practices in our society and to create new ways of knowing, different strategies for the sharing of knowledge. (p. 12)

We have our work cut out for us. Our challenge is to work not only with those who agree with us, but also with those who see the situation very differently, and most of all with people who are giving up, tired of the struggle. A line in Alice Walker's (1984) poem "Each One, Pull One" speaks to our task: *"Each one, pull one back into the sun.... "* In order to move forward into a world that values all of us, both because we are human and also because of the differences that make us who we are, each of us must take individual and institutional responsibility for creating education in which all children will thrive.

Appendix A

Bibliography of Books on Multicultural Issues for Adults

Allen, Paula Gunn. *The Sacred Hoop: Recovering the Feminine in American Indian Traditions.* Boston: Beacon Press, 1992.

　Gunn, a Laguna Pueblo/Sioux Indian, describes the pivotal role women play in Native American history and spiritual life.

Andersen, M. L., & Collins, Patricia Hill. *Race, Class, and Gender: An Anthology.* Belmont, CA: Wadsworth Publishing Company, 1995.

　The articles in this anthology address the connections between race, class, and gender. They also present a variety of perspectives on families, sexuality, American identity, empowerment and change.

Anson, Robert Sam. *Best Intentions: The Education and Killing of Edmund Perry.* New York: Random House, 1987.

　The summer after Edmund Perry, a young African American man identified as "Harlem's prized symbol of hope," graduated from Phillips Exeter Academy, he was shot to death in Manhattan by a police officer. His is the story of cultural schizophrenia, the result of trying to be successful and Black in White America. It is definitely a book that gives us pause.

Augenbraum, Harold, & Stavans, Ilan, Eds. *Growing Up Latino.* Boston: Houghton Mifflin, 1993.

　This anthology is a compilation of coming-of-age stories by Latinas and Latinos living in the United States. The stories are written by many of the most prominent Hispanic writers in the country.

Bell, Derrick. *Faces at the Bottom of the Well: The Permanence of Racism.* New York: Basic Books, 1992.

　Bell is one of the nation's most prominent law professors. In this book he writes powerfully about the ways in which racism defines all our lives.

Bennett, Lerone. *Before the Mayflower: A History of Black America,* 6th Rev. ed. New York: Viking, 1993.
> Lerone Bennett's important and comprehensive history of African Americans in the United States fills in some of the gaps in information about Black people's role in American history.

Branch, Taylor. *Parting the Waters: America in the King Years, 1954–1963.* New York: Simon & Schuster, 1988.
> Awarded a Pulitzer prize for nonfiction, this is, in some ways, a personal history of the civil-rights movement. Branch focuses on the life of Martin Luther King and those whom he touched, both famous and unknown.

Brown, Dee. *Bury My Heart at Wounded Knee: An Indian History of the American West.* New York: Holt & Company, 1991.
> This is a landmark book that tells—from an Indian perspective—about White people's destruction of American Indian civilization and culture.

Clark, Don. *The New Loving Someone Gay.* Berkeley, CA: Celestial Arts, 1990.
> Clark provides basic guidance and information for those who are gay and/or for those who love someone gay. His approach is straightforward and upbeat.

Cose, Ellis. *The Rage of a Privileged Class.* New York: HarperCollins, 1993.
> Cose writes about the experience of middle- and upper-middle-class African Americans in the United States today. Believed by Whites to have been able to "move beyond race" because of their economic class, interviewees describe the ways in which racism continues to affect their lives daily.

Delpit, Lisa. *Other People's Children: Cultural Conflict in the Classroom.* New York: The New Press, 1995.
> These essays probe basic assumptions on which much of contemporary education is based. Delpit asserts that culture clashes between White teachers and children of color are hindering children's success in schools. Her writing is exciting and thought-provoking.

Fairchild, Betty, & Hayward, Nancy. *Now that You Know: What Every Parent Should Know about Homosexuality.* New York: Harcourt Brace Jovanovich, 1989.
> Both of the authors of this book are mothers of gay children. They have written a down-to-earth, sympathetic, and enlightening book for parents of gay men and lesbians. Stages of responding to having a gay child are discussed, as are issues of religion and AIDS.

Faludi, Susan. *Backlash: The Undeclared War Against American Women.* New York: Crown Publishers, 1991.
> This is a disturbing exploration of the ways in which women's "progress" toward equal rights is being eroded. Faludi discusses incident after incident in the war against women in the media, popular culture, politics, and the corporate culture.

Frankenberg, Ruth. *White Women, Race Matters: The Social Construction of Whiteness.* Minneapolis: University of Minnesota Press, 1993.
> Though academic in tone, Frankenberg argues forcefully that race shapes the experiences of White women. Through interviews, she explores the issues of the social geography of race, interracial couples, and interracial parenting.

Giddings, Paula. *When and Where I Enter: The Impact of Black Women on Race and Sex in America*. New York: Bantam, 1985.
> While this was published earlier than most of the books in this bibliography, it stills holds an important place in documenting the history of African American women, and the intersection of racism and sexism in American history.

Gould, Stephen Jay. *The Mismeasure of Man*. New York: W. W. Norton, 1981.
> With the resurgence of discussion of the "scientific" research on the connections between race and intelligence, prompted by the publication of *The Bell Curve* (Robert Herrnstein & Charles Murray, New York: Free Press, 1994), Gould's book becomes all the more important. He exposes the flaws in the original research, and shows how it has been used as an excuse for the treatment that people of color have historically received in this country.

Hacker, Andrew. *Two Nations*. New York: Charles Scribner's Sons, 1992.
> Hacker's study of the conditions of Blacks and Whites in present-day United States is distressing. He finds that the myth of Black inferiority and White superiority is at the root of ongoing racism, and that one of its consequences is that Black people are kept out of the American economy.

Heath, Shirley Brice. *Ways with Words*. New York: Cambridge University Press, 1983.
> In this fascinating book, Heath reports on her research on language, race, and socioeconomic class. She studies language usage in two working-class communities: "Trackton," a Black community, and "Roadville," a White community. In reading it, the root of some of the "culture clashes" that Delpit discusses begin to make sense.

hooks, bell. *Talking Back*. Boston: South End Press, 1989.

hooks, bell. *Yearning*. Boston: South End Press, 1990.

hooks, bell. *Teaching to Transgress*. New York: Routledge, 1994.
> These are three of my favorite books by bell hooks. In *Talking Back*, hooks looks at recovery of the self, White supremacy, and at being a Black feminist. In *Yearning*, she addresses the intersections of race and gender as she writes about Black women and men, whiteness, cultural politics, and choosing to live in the margin. *Teaching to Transgress* is about the "practice of freedom," as Paulo Friere called the process of education. hooks believes that it is the teacher's responsibility to help their students deal with racism and sexism in the classroom.

Katz, Judy. *White Awareness*. Norman, Oklahoma: University of Oklahoma Press, 1978.
> When it was published, this book quickly became one of the most widely used in the field of racism-awareness training. It is still extremely useful as a handbook for White people who are interested in understanding personal and institutional racism.

Kotlowitz, Alex. *There Are No Children Here*. New York: Doubleday, 1991.
> Kotlowitz met Lafayette and Pharoah Rivers when he was doing a story on children living in poverty in Chicago. He became interested in them and decided to write their story as a way of putting urban poverty— or as Michael Harrington called it, *The Other America*—in the minds and hearts of middle-class Americans. This is a book about endurance, survival, and triumph.

Lakoff, Robin. *Talking Power: The Politics of Language.* New York: Basic Books, 1990.
There are many books that address the process and content of communication. Robin Lakoff is clearer about the role that power plays in our interactions than any other linguist. Her work is invaluable.

Lerner, Gerda, Ed. *Black Women in White America.* New York: Vintage Books, 1988.
More than 20 years after it was originally published, this book still provides
fascinating and important reading. It is a unique collection of documents—
letters, statements, articles, manuscripts—written by American women, mostly
Black, from 1870 to 1970.

Lim, Shirley Geok-lin, Tsutakawa, Mayumi, & Donnelly, Margarita. *The Forbidden Stitch:
An Asian American Women's Anthology.* Corvallis, OR: Calyx Books, 1989.
Unless we happen to live near Asian American communities, most of us know
very little about Asian American women. This is a collection of poetry, art, fic-
tion, and autobiographical pieces by women around the country.

Mallory, Bruce L., & New, Rebecca S., Eds. *Diversity and Developmentally Appropriate
Practices.* New York: Teachers College Press, 1994.
The essays included in this book are important, provocative, and firmly rooted in theory. The authors push us to look with a fresh eye at what is problematic about prescribing practices that are appropriate for "all" children.

McCarthy, Cameron, & Crichlow, Warren, Eds. *Race Identity and Representation in Education.* New York: Routledge, 1993.
The editors of this volume of essays intend it to be a "strategic intervention"
that moves the reader to rethink issues of race and identity. Included are articles titled "Children and the Grammar of Popular Racism," "How White
Teachers Construct Race," and "I Pledge Allegiance: The Politics of Reading
and Using Educational Films."

Muse, Daphne, Ed. *Prejudice: Stories about Hate, Ignorance, Revelation, and Transforma-
tion.* New York: Hyperion Books for Children, 1995.
Included in this group of stories are works by Lynda Barry, Sandra Cisneros,
Flannery O'Connor, and Ntozake Shange. Each looks at prejudice in its
unique way.

Nieto, Sonia. *Affirming Diversity: The Sociopolitical Context of Multicultural Education.*
(2nd ed.). New York: Longman, 1995.
Nieto places her work on multicultural education in the sociopolitical arena.
Believing that it is neither wise nor possible to separate school from the world,
she addresses both the meaning of multicultural education and the "structur-
al factors" in school that work against student success.

Orenstein, Peggy. *School Girls: Young Women, Self-Esteem, and the Confidence Gap.* New
York: Doubleday, 1994.
When the American Association of University Women conducted their study
on young women in high schools and colleges around the country, Peggy
Orenstein talked with the individual people involved. She has produced a
poignant, and at times anger-provoking, compilation of their voices and a
commentary on their thoughts.

Paley, Vivian Gussin. *Kwanzaa and Me.* Cambridge: Harvard University Press, 1995.
In her seventh book about teaching young children, Paley, a White woman,

works to understand why African Americans would want to put their children in all-Black schools. Her writing is extremely accessible; thus the complicated issue also becomes more easily approached.

Pipher, Mary. *Reviving Ophelia: Saving the Selves of Adolescent Girls.* New York: Ballantine Books, 1994.

This is a heart-rending book about what happens to girls as they grow into adolescence. Pipher, a therapist who has worked with adolescent girls for years, tells us that suicide, anorexia, and bulimia are all products of what happens to young girls in our culture. She also discusses what we might do to save girls in trouble.

Sadker, Myra, & Sadker, David. *Failing at Fairness: How Our Schools Cheat Girls.* New York: Simon & Schuster, 1994.

For over twenty years, the Sadkers have been doing research on gender bias. Their newest work looks at the ways that girls' school experiences are far less positive than boys' and the effects of those experiences on later life.

Silin, Jonathan G. *Sex, Death, and the Education of Children: Our Passion for Ignorance in the Age of AIDS.* New York: Teachers College Press, 1995.

In this ground-breaking book, Jonathan Silin combines what he knows about the AIDS epidemic and about early-childhood education—his personal and professional lives. Deftly melding the two, he moves the reader to understand that adults fail to teach children what they themselves are afraid to know. Our fantasy is that we are protecting children by not raising questions that might be "troubling"; in fact, it is the adults who are disturbed by complex conversations. This is a wonderful book.

Sleeter, Christine. *Keepers of the American Dream.* Bristol, PA: The Falmer Press, 1992.

Sleeter reports on a 2-year ethnographic study of thirty teachers involved in staff development in multicultural education. She finds that changes in the subjects' teaching following the staff development were limited, and she offers analysis of why that is the case and what needs to occur to bring about change.

Sleeter, Christine, & Grant, Carl. *Making Choices for Multicultural Education: Five Approaches to Race, Class, and Gender* (2nd ed.). New York: Macmillan, 1994.

Sleeter and Grant believe that many different approaches are taken to education under the rubric of "multicultural education." In response, they have developed a helpful typology of five approaches, with each one's goals and related activities. This is useful in gaining clarity about where you want to go and how to get there.

Smith, Lillian. *Killers of the Dream.* New York: Norton, 1978.

Lillian Smith is a White woman who grew up in the South. She writes, in this autobiography, about the racism in the South and its effect on her.

Storm, Hyemeyohsts. *Seven Arrows.* New York: Ballantine, 1972.

Twenty years after its publication, this book about the Plains Indians, the Medicine Wheel, and our place in the universe has lost none of its power.

Takaki, Ronald. *A Different Mirror: A History of Multicultural America.* Boston: Little, Brown and Company, 1993.

This is a history of America from the perspective of its non-Anglo citizens:

Irish, Jews, African Americans, Native Americans, Asian Americans, and Latinos. In it, Takaki tells not only of the contributions made by minority peoples
but also of their struggle for justice.

Takaki, Ronald. *Strangers from a Different Shore: A History of Asian Americans*. New York:
Penguin, 1990.

In this book, Ronald Takaki has written a history of Asians, their immigration
to America, and their experiences here.

Tannen, Deborah. *You Just Don't Understand*. New York: William Morrow and Company, 1990.

It is not a secret that men and women are often unable to communicate; what
is still unclear is why. Tannen addresses the disconnections in male–female
communication in hopes of raising awareness in both genders.

Terkel, Studs. *Race: How Blacks and Whites Think and Feel About the American Obsession*.
New York: The New Press, 1992.

In his inimitable style, Terkel interviews White people and African Americans
around the country on their ideas about race. The book is both accessible and
powerful.

Weis, Lois, & Fein, Michelle, Eds. *Beyond Silenced Voices: Class, Race, & Gender in United States Schools*. Albany: State University of New York Press, 1993.

This is a strong collection of articles about class, race, and gender in schools.
Note particularly "Choices, Not Closets: Heterosexism and Homophobia in
Schools" by Richard Friend.

West, Cornel. *Race Matters*. Boston: Beacon Press, 1993.

In the midst of a time when many argue that race doesn't and/or shouldn't
matter, Cornel West argues forcefully about its impact on our daily lives. If you
read only the preface, I believe you will be moved.

Whitlock, Katherine. *Bridges of Respect: Creating Support for Lesbian and Gay Youth* (Rev.
ed.). Philadelphia: American Friends Service Committee, 1989.

Teachers will be helped by this straightforward book on supporting young
gays and lesbians. As one might expect from a publication of the American
Friends Service Committee, the focus is on building respect among young
people.

Williams, Patricia J. The Alchemy of Race and Rights. Cambridge, MA; Harvard
University Press, 1991.

Patricia Williams deftly uses the intricacies of racism in the law to explore the
experience of people of color in the mid-1990s. This is essential reading for
those who want to gain a deeper understanding of the effects of institutional
racism on individuals.

Appendix B

Bibliography of
Multicultural Children's Books

Adoff, Arnold. *All Kinds of Families*. New York: Morrow, 1992.
> These poems deal with the feelings of a biracial child.

Adoff, Arnold. *Black Is Brown Is Tan*. Illus. by Emily A. McCully. New York: Harper & Row, 1973.
> This is a story–poem about a racially mixed family.

Adoff, Arnold. *Flamboyan*. Illus. by Karen Barbour. San Diego, CA: Harcourt Brace Jovanovich, 1988.
> On a Caribbean island, a baby is born. Her parents name her Flamboyan, after a strong, colorful tree. We follow Flamboyan through her natural "seasons."

Ahenakew, Freda. *How the Birch Tree Got Its Stripes*. Illus. by George Littlefield. Saskatoon: Fifth House, 1988.
> In this traditional "how it came to be" story, Wishkecahk attempts to prove himself strong, finds out he isn't, and takes it out on the birch trees.

Aliki. *Corn Is Maize*. New York: Crowell, 1976.
> This simple, factual book is about corn: the life cycle of the corn plant and the development of it as a food source.

Altman, Linda J. *Amelia's Road*. Illus. by Enrique O. Sanchez. New York: Lee & Low Books, 1993.
> Amelia and her family are migrant workers. Amelia dreams of a place where she can stay forever and finds a special road by which she can always return.

Archambault, John, & Martin, Bill, Jr. *Knots on a Counting Rope*. Illus. by Ted Rand. New York: Henry Holt and Company, 1987.
> Boy-Strength-of-Blue-Horses learns the story of his birth from his grandfather,

who ties another knot in the counting rope every time he tells it. As time passes, the boy gains the courage and confidence to face life's challenges—including his blindness.

Aseltine, Lorraine, & Mueller, E. *I'm Deaf and It's Okay.* Chicago: Albert Whitman, 1986.

A hearing-impaired teenager helps a young child come to terms with his own impairment.

Ashley, Bernard. *Cleversticks.* Illus. by Derek Brazell. New York: Crown, 1992.

Ling Sung is unhappy at his English preschool until he discovers a unique skill that everyone wants to learn.

Atkinson, Mary. *Maria Teresa* (2d ed.). Carrboro, NC: Lollipop Power, 1979.

Maria Teresa, a young Latina, must learn to deal with the discrimination she encounters in a Midwestern city.

Avery, Charles E. *Everybody Has Feelings/Todos Tenemos Sentimientos.* Seattle, WA: Open Hand Publishing, 1992.

This book, in Spanish and in English, talks about feelings.

Bales, Carol Ann. *Kevin Cloud: Chippewa Boy in the City.* Chicago: Reilly & Lee, 1972.

Told in photographs, this bilingual story explores the many moods of childhood through Kevin Cloud, a Native American who lives in Chicago.

Bang, Molly. *The Paper Crane.* New York: Greenwillow Books, 1987.

A Japanese American man brings a magic paper crane to life.

Bang, Molly. *Ten, Nine, Eight.* New York: Greenwillow Books, 1983.

A father puts his young daughter to bed, counting backwards as she gets ready.

Banish, Roslyn. *A Forever Family.* New York: HarperCollins, 1992.

Eight-year-old Jennifer tells about being adopted into a "forever family" after living in several foster homes. Multiracial families are depicted.

Baylor, Byrd. *Amigo.* Illus. by Garth Williams. New York: Macmillan, 1989.

Desperately wanting a pet to love, a boy decides to tame a prairie dog who has already decided to tame the boy as his own pet.

Baylor, Byrd. *The Best Town in the World.* Illus. by Ronald Himler. New York: Macmillan, 1983.

This is a nostalgic view of a town in which dogs were smarter, chickens laid prettier eggs, wildflowers grew taller and thicker, and the people knew how to make the best chocolate cakes and toys in the world.

Baylor, Byrd. *The Desert Is Theirs.* Illus. by Peter Parnall. New York: Macmillan, 1975.

The simple text and illustrations describe and show the characteristics of the desert and its plant, animal, and human life.

Baylor, Byrd. *Everybody Needs a Rock.* Illus. by Peter Parnall. New York: Macmillan, 1974.

This book discusses the qualities to consider in selecting the perfect rock for play and pleasure.

Baylor, Byrd. *Guess Who My Favorite Person Is.* Illus. by Robert Andrew Parker. New York: Macmillan, 1992.

Two friends play the game of naming their favorite things.

Baylor, Byrd. *Hawk, I'm Your Brother.* Illus. by Peter Parnall. New York: Macmillan, 1976.

A young boy who lives in the desert steals a baby hawk from its nest, hoping that he, too, can learn to fly.

Baylor, Byrd. *If You Are a Hunter of Fossils.* Illus. by Peter Parnall. New York: Macmillan, 1980.
> A geologist looking for signs of an ancient sea in the rocks of a western Texas mountain shows how the area must have looked millions of years ago.

Baylor, Byrd. *The Way to Start a Day.* Illus. by Peter Parnall. New York: Macmillan, 1986.
> The text and illustrations show how people all over the world celebrate the sunrise.

Baylor, Byrd. *When Clay Sings.* Illus. by Tom Bahti. New York: Macmillan, 1987.
> The daily life and customs of prehistoric Southwest Indian tribes are revealed through the designs on the remains of their pottery.

Beller, Janet. *A–B–C-ing: An Action Alphabet.* New York: Crown, 1984.
> Children in photographs enact an action word for each letter of the alphabet, from *acting* to *marching* to *zipping*.

Bosche, Susanne. *Jenny Lives with Eric and Martin.* London: Gay Men's Press, 1983.
> Together, the members of a gay family in London experience prejudice and openly discuss their feelings.

Bruchac, Joseph. *Fox Song.* Illus. by Paul Morin. New York: Philomel Books, 1993.
> Although Grama Bowman is gone, Jamie's quiet walk in the woods tells her that her grandmother is still near.

Bunin, Catherine, & Bunin, Sherry. *Is That Your Sister? A True Story of Adoption.* Wayne, PA: Our Child Press, 1992.
> An adopted 6-year-old girl tells about adoption and how she and her adopted sister feel about it.

Bunnett, Rochelle. *Friends in the Park.* New York: Checkerboard Press Inc., 1993.
> This book shows differently-abled children enjoying everyday fun with their friends.

Bunting, Eve. *Fly Away Home.* Illus. by Ronald Himler. New York: Clarion Books, 1991.
> A little boy and his father, the Medinas, are homeless and live surreptitiously at the airport. The father works days and tries to save enough money for a more stable home. Other homeless people also live at the airport and create a kind of family with the Medinas.

Bunting, Eve. *St. Patrick's Day in the Morning.* New York: Clarion Books, 1983.
> In Ireland, a child sets out to prove he is big enough to march in the St. Patrick's Day parade.

Caines, Jeanette Franklin. *Abby.* Illus. by Steven Kellogg. New York: Harper & Row, 1973.
> Abby is a young Black girl who is adopted. The story centers on her relationships with her adoptive parents and brother Kevin.

Caines, Jeanette Franklin. *Daddy.* New York: Harper & Row, 1977.
> This is the story of an African American father and daughter.

Caines, Jeanette Franklin. *I Need a Lunch Box.* Illus. by Pat Cummings. New York: Harper & Row, 1988.
> As school is about to begin, the younger brother in an African American family dreams of what he would do if he had his own lunch box.

Caines, Jeanette Franklin. *Just Us Women.* Illus. by Pat Cummings. New York: Harper & Row, 1982.
> An African American girl and her aunt take a car trip together to North Carolina.

Caines, Jeanette Franklin. *Window Wishing*. Illus. by Kevin Brooks. New York: Harper & Row, 1980.
> This is the story of two Black children spending their vacation with their grandmother.

Cairo, Shelly, Cairo, Jasmine, & Cairo, Tara. *Our Brother Has Down's Syndrome*. Toronto: Annick Press, 1985.
> Two sisters tell about their little brother Jai, who has Down's Syndrome.

Cameron, A. *Spider Woman*. Madiera Park, BC: Harbour, 1988.
> This is the tale of a legendary figure in the belief system of the Navajos.

Cherry, Lynne. *The Great Kapok Tree*. San Diego, CA: Harcourt Brace, 1990.
> A man intends to cut down a tree in the Amazon rain forest, but is persuaded to let it live by all the creatures that depend on the tree.

Children's Television Workshop. *Sign Language Fun*. New York: Random House, 1980.
> This beginning book in signing teaches children some of the basic words and phrases.

Church, Vivian. *Colors Around Me*. Chicago: Afro-American Publishing, 1971.
> A book for all ages: it explains the variety of skin tones among African Americans.

Clifton, Lucille. *Amifika*. Illus. by Thomas DiGrazia. New York: Dutton, 1977.
> This is a story for very young children about a father's return from the armed services.

Clifton, Lucille. *Don't You Remember?* Illus. by Evaline Ness. New York: Dutton, 1973.
> There is a happy ending to this story of a working-class African American family in which 4-year-old Tate negotiates her way in a life of broken promises.

Clifton, Lucille. *Everett Anderson's Friend*. Illus. by Lucille Clifton. New York: Holt, Rinehart & Winston, 1992.
> Everett Anderson, a young Black boy, forgets his key, and, when he is invited into the house of the Hispanic girl who has just moved next door, they become friends.

Clifton, Lucille. *Everett Anderson's Goodbye*. Illus. by Ann Grifalconi. New York: Holt, Rinehart & Winston, 1988.
> An African American family loses the father. Everett moves through stages of grief with the help of his mother. The story is told in verse.

Clifton, Lucille. *Everett Anderson's Nine Month Long*. Illus. by Ann Grifalconi. New York: Holt, Rinehart & Winston, 1978.
> Everett Anderson notices changes in his mother and in their home and finds out about the baby that is about to be born.

Clifton, Lucille. *Some of the Days of Everett Anderson*. Illus. by Evaline Ness. New York: Holt, Rinehart & Winston, 1970.
> This Everett Anderson book is a collection of short poems about Everett and the city in which he lives.

Cohen, Miriam. *Will I Have a Friend?* Illus. by Lillian Hoban. New York: Macmillan, 1967.
> This is the story of a young child's first day in kindergarten.

Connexion, Ruth A. *Friday Night Is Papa Night*. Illus. by Emily A. McCulley. New York: Puffin Books, 1987.
> Friday night is the family's special night because Papa joins them, but this week Papa doesn't come home.

Corey, Dorothy. *You Go Away.* New York: Greenwillow Book, 1993.
> This story of a multiracial family depicts the supportive roles of both parents. In the end, the family must face a separation.

Cowen-Fletcher, Jane. *Mama Zooms.* New York: Scholastic, Inc., 1993.
> This story is about a little boy who zooms around with his mother, who uses a wheelchair.

Crews, Donald. *Bigmama's.* New York: Greenwillow Books, 1991.
> Years later, an African American man describes all the pleasures of the annual family trip to Bigmama's homestead in Florida. Bigmama is his grandmother, one of a large extended family of rural working-class relatives and friends.

Crews, Donald. *Shortcut.* New York: Greenwillow Books, 1988.
> The children of *Bigmama's* take a forbidden shortcut along a railroad track.

Cummings, Pat. *Clean Up Your Room, Harvey Moon.* Scarsdale, NY: Bradbury Press, 1991.
> This is the verse story of Harvey, an African American boy, whose room is a mess and who can't watch TV until he cleans it.

Daly, Niki. *Not So Fast Songololo.* New York: Atheneum, 1986.
> Malusi, a Black South African boy, spends a shopping day with his grandmother.

Davol, Marguerite W. *Black, White, Just Right.* Illus. by Irene Trivas. New York: Four Winds, 1993.
> A biracial child tells about her family and the fun they have together.

DeGrosbois, L., Lacelle, N., LaMothe, R., & Nantel, L. *Mommy Works on Dresses.* Toronto: Women's Press, 1976.
> This is the story of a family whose mother works in a dress factory.

dePaola, Tomie. *The Legend of the Bluebonnet.* New York: Putnam, 1981.
> A Native American girl has a favorite doll which she finally gives up so that the entire tribe can benefit from the rain.

dePaola, Tomie. *Nana Upstairs, Nana Downstairs.* New York: Putnam, 1973.

dePaola, Tomie. *Now One Foot, Now the Other.* New York: Putnam, 1980.
> Two stories depicting loving family relationships between generations.

dePaola, Tomie. *Oliver Button Is a Sissy.* New York: Harcourt Brace Jovanovich, 1979.
> Oliver gets teased by his classmates because he doesn't like to play the kinds of games that boys usually play. He loves to dance and, when he performs in a talent show, his classmates discover how good Oliver is at being his natural self.

dePaola, Tomie. *Watch Out for the Chicken Feet in Your Soup.* Englewood Cliffs, NJ: Prentice-Hall, 1974.
> Joey takes his friend to visit his Old-World Italian grandmother and learns that her foreign accent and cultural differences can be interesting and appreciated rather than being ridiculed.

Dooley, Norah. *Everybody Cooks Rice.* Minneapolis, MN: Carolrhoda Books, 1991.
> Visiting homes in her neighborhood, a young girl finds rice being cooked in a number of different ways. Recipes are included.

Dorros, Arthur. *Abuela.* New York: Dutton Children's Books, 1991.
> This fantasy is about a girl and her grandmother flying over the sights of New York City. A glossary of Spanish words is included.

Dorros, Arthur. *Radio Man.* New York: HarperCollins, 1993.
> In this story of a migrant Latino family, young Diego finds the radio a com-

panion, a good source for bilingual information, and a tool for keeping in
touch with his friend David.

Dragonwagon, Crescent. *Always, Always.* New York: Macmillan, 1984.
   A young child experiences divorce in the family and then the predicament of
   shared custody.

Drescher, Joan. *Your Family, My Family.* New York: Walker & Co., 1980.
   This book briefly describes several kinds of families and cites some of the
   strengths of family life.

Elwin, Rosamund, & Paulse, Michele. *Asha's Mums.* Illus. by Dawn Lee. Toronto:
Women's Press, 1990.
   Asha learns that her teacher doesn't understand about her two "mums." Her
   diverse classmates share their views, and her mothers come to school. Everyone learns that you can, in fact, have two wonderful mothers.

Fassler, Joan. *My Grandpa Died Today.* New York: Human Sciences Press, 1983.
   A Jewish family deals with the death of their patriarch.

Feelings, Muriel. *Jambo Means Hello: Swahili Alphabet Book.* Illus. by Tom Feelings. New
York: Dial Press, 1971.
   This is a picture book with simple text and easy beginning phrases in Swahili.

Feelings, Tom. *Moja Means One: A Swahili Counting Book.* New York: Dial Press, 1973.
   In this illustrated counting book, the numbers from one to ten are given in
   English and Swahili.

Feelings, Tom, (Ed.), *Soul Looks Back in Wonder.* Illus. by the editor. New York: Dial
Books, 1993.
   A collection of poems about African American roots in Africa. Poems by Mari
   Evans, Maya Angelou, and Langston Hughes are included.

Fox, Mem. *Wilfred Gordon McDonald Partridge.* Illus. by Julie Vivas. Brooklyn, NY:
Kane/Miller Book Publishers, 1989.
   This story from Australia is about a small boy and his friendships with people
   in a retirement home next door.

Freeman, Don. *Corduroy.* New York: Viking Press, 1965.
   A young Black girl finds the teddy bear, Corduroy, in a busy department store.

Freeney, Stephanie. *Hawaii Is a Rainbow.* Honolulu: University of Hawaii Press, 1980.
   Hawaii comes to life in this picture book with color photographs.

Friedman, Ina R. *How My Parents Learned to Eat.* Illus. by Allen Say. Boston: Houghton
Mifflin, 1987.
   A young girl tells how her Japanese mother and American father met and
   adapted to each other's cultures.

Girrard, Linda W., & Levine, Abby, (Eds.). *Adoption Is for Always.* Chicago: Albert
Whitman, 1986.
   This book relates the feelings and experiences of a child who finds out she's
   adopted.

Goble, Paul. *The Friendly Wolf.* Scarsdale, NY: Bradbury Press, 1975.
   Two Native American children, separated from their family, are befriended
   and helped to get home by a wolf.

Goble, Paul. *The Girl Who Loved Wild Horses.* Scarsdale, NY: Bradbury Press, 1978.
   A young Native American girl loves to ride with the wild horses even more
   than being with her family and tribe.

Golenbock, Peter. *Teammates*. San Diego, CA: Harcourt Brace Jovanovich, 1990.
This is the story of the breaking of the color barrier in baseball by Jackie Robinson in 1947. It is a tribute to Robinson and two White men, Branch Rickey and "Pee Wee" Reese, who stood with him. The book is illustrated with drawings and vintage photographs.

Greenburg, Polly. *I Know I'm Myself Because*. New York: Human Sciences Press, 1986.
This is a story of a young girl and her mother, both happy and well-adjusted; the father is not mentioned.

Greenburg, Polly. *Rosie and Roo*. Washington, DC: The Growth Program Press, 1988.
This is a story about a family composed of two mothers, two children, one grandmother, and no fathers.

Greenfield, Eloise. *Africa Dream*. Illus. by Carole Byard. New York: John Day, 1977.
In this fantasy, a young Black girl dreams about being in Africa.

Greenfield, Eloise. *Grandpa's Face*. Illus. by Floyd Cooper. New York: Philomel Books, 1993.
This books depicts the enduring love between a child and her grandfather.

Greenfield, Eloise. *Honey I Love and Other Poems*. Illus. by Diane and Leo Dillon. New York: Crowell, 1986.
This is a collection of love poems written especially for children.

Greenfield, Eloise. *Me and Nessie*. Illus. by Moneta Barnett. New York: Crowell, 1975.
This picture book tells the story of a young Black girl, her family, her imaginary friend Nessie, and her first day at school.

Greenfield, Eloise. *Night on Neighborhood Street*. Illus. by Jan Spivey Gilchrist. New York: Dial Press, 1991.
These illustrated poems are about life on Neighborhood Street. They cover a range of experiences from a father losing his job to kids encountering drug dealers to the birth of a baby sister.

Greenfield, Eloise. *Rosa Parks*. New York: Crowell, 1973.
This is a brief biography of the Black woman, often called the Mother of the Civil Rights Movement, who started the Montgomery bus boycott.

Greenfield, Eloise. *William and the Good Old Days*. Illus. by Jan Spivey Gilchrist. New York: Crowell, 1993.
William misses the "good old days" when his grandmother was not sick and they could have fun together.

Grimes, Nikki. *Meet Danitra Brown*. Illus. by Floyd Cooper. New York: Lothrop, Lee & Shepard, 1994.
Two little African American girls have big spirits, great experiences, and a fiercely loyal friendship. Thirteen poems in the voice of one of them sing of adventure, single parents, courage, fun, and pride.

Grimes, Nikki. *Something on My Mind*. Illus. by Tom Feelings. New York: Dial Press, 1978.
This book of poems for all children deals with the problems of being a child in our world.

Hamilton, Virginia. *The People Could Fly: American Black Folktales*. Illus. by Leo & Diane Dillon. New York: Knopf, 1985.
These 24 selections from traditional Black American folklore include tricksters tales, tall tales, ghost tales, and tales of freedom.

Havehill, Juanita. *Jamaica and Brianna.* Illus. by Ann Sibley O'Brien. Boston: Houghton Mifflin, 1993.
> A story about two friends who hurt each other's feelings, but are able to resolve their differences.

Hayes, Sarah. *Eat Up, Gemma.* Illus. by Jan Ormerod. New York: Lothrop, Lee & Shepard, 1988.
> Baby Gemma refuses to eat, throwing her breakfast on the floor and squashing her grapes, until her brother gets an idea.

Hazen, Barbara S. *Tight Times.* New York: Viking Children's Books, 1979.
> This is the story of a boy who wants a dog, a father who loses his job, and a family that figures out how to cope without much money.

Hazen, Barbara S. *Why Are People Different? A Book About Prejudice.* New York: Golden Books, 1985.
> A grandparent helps teach a young child about prejudice.

Heide, Florence Parry, & Gilliland, Judith Heide. *The Day of Ahmed's Secret.* New York: Lothrop, Lee & Shepard, 1990.
> We follow Ahmed through his day in Cairo: his chores, his observations, the sights and sounds of the city. He carries around a secret all day and finally shares it with his loving family.

Henriod, Lorraine. *Grandma's Wheelchair.* Chicago: Albert Whitman, 1982.
> This book describes a day with Thomas and his grandmother and the fun they have with her wheelchair.

Highwater, Jamake. *Moonsong Lullaby.* New York: Lothrop, Lee & Shepard, 1981.
> This is a poetic story of nature and the Ancestors, told to a Native American child of the People. It is illustrated with color photographs.

Hirsch, Marilyn. *I Love Hanukkah.* New York: Holiday House, 1984.
> A young boy describes his family's celebration of Hanukkah and the things he likes about the holiday.

Hirsch, Marilyn. *Potato Pancakes All Around: A Hanukkah Tale.* New York: Bonhim Books, 1978.
> This humorous story celebrates some of the traditions of Hanukkah.

Hitte, Kathryn. *Mexicali Soup.* Illus. by Anne Rockwell. New York: Parents Magazine Press, 1970.
> In this Chicago family, Mama is glad to be in a big city where she can get the best ingredients for her Mexicali soup. Her children, however, are embarrassed about the soup and try to get Mama to change the recipe. The book offers a lesson about trying too hard to adapt to another culture.

Hoban, Russell. *Bedtime for Frances.* Illus. by Garth Williams. New York: Harper and Row, 1960.
> Frances has lots of excuses for not wanting to go to bed. Her father convinces her it is her job.

Hoban, Russell. *Bread and Jam for Frances.* Illus. by Lillian Hoban. New York: Scholastic, 1964.
> Frances the badger only wants to eat bread and jam until her mother tells her that's all she can eat.

Hoffman, Mary. *Amazing Grace.* Illus. by Caroline Binch. New York: Dial Books, 1991.

Who says an African American girl can't play Peter Pan? Grace learns she can be what she wants to be, especially with her talent and imagination.

Hudson, Wade, (Ed.). *Pass It On: African American Poetry for Children*. Illus. by Floyd Cooper. New York: Scholastic Inc., 1993.

Fourteen African American poets are represented in this anthology of poetry for young children.

Hurwitz, Johanna. *New Shoes for Silvia*. Illus. by Jerry Pinkney. New York: Morrow Junior Books, 1993.

Silvia has received a gift of beautiful red shoes from Tia Rosita, but Silvia needs to grow into them.

Isadora, Rachel. *At the Crossroads*. New York: Greenwillow Books, 1991.

This is a story about South African children waiting for their fathers to return from working in the mine.

Isadora, Rachel. *Ben's Trumpet*. New York: Greenwillow Books, 1979.

A young Black child in an urban neighborhood loves the music of the trumpet player in a nearby jazz club.

Johnston, Tony. *The Quilt Story*. Illus. by Tomie dePaola. New York: Putnam, 1985.

A quilt passed down for generations provides comfort to each new child who discovers it.

Joose, Barbara. *Mama, Do You Love Me?* Illus. by Barbara Lavallee. San Francisco: Chronicle Books, 1991.

An Alaskan child tests the mother's limits and love. The book includes references to and illustrations of Arctic animals and Inuit culture.

Kasza, Keiko. *A Mother for Choco*. New York: Putnam, 1992.

A little bird lives all alone and looks for his mother. After much rejection, Choco finally finds Mrs. Bear who has all the qualities of the best adoptive mother.

Keats, Ezra. *Apt. 3*. New York: Macmillan, 1971.

Two small children explore their apartment building.

Keats, Ezra. *Goggles*. New York: Macmillan, 1969.

Two young boys outwit a gang of older boys.

Keats, Ezra. *Hi, Cat!* New York: Macmillan, 1972.

This is another Keats story about two inner-city boys and a stray cat.

Keats, Ezra. *A Letter to Amy*. New York: Harper & Row, 1968.

Peter's birthday party would be all boys if it weren't for Amy.

Keats, Ezra. *Pet Show!* New York: Macmillan, 1972.

A pet show brings together many children and their pets, even young Archie who can't find his cat to enter him in the show.

Keats, Ezra. *Peter's Chair*. New York: Harper & Row, 1967.

Peter has trouble getting used to his new role as a big brother until he realizes that he has special privileges and abilities because of his age and size.

Keats, Ezra. *The Snowy Day*. New York: Scholastic, 1967.

Peter has an adventurous day playing in the snow.

Keats, Ezra. *Whistle for Willie*. New York: Viking Press, 1964.

This is a picture book of a child's solitary play and beginning attempts at whistling.

Klein, Norma. *Girls Can Be Anything*. New York: Dutton, 1975.
> Marina, a curious and energetic girl, confronts her school friend, Adam, on his limited and limiting ideas of what girls can do and be when they grow up.

Krauss, Ruth. *The Carrot Seed*. New York: HarperCollins Children's Books, 1993.
> This is a perfectly wonderful book about a child who persists and triumphs in spite of discouragement from those around him.

Kroll, Virginia. *African Brothers and Sisters*. Chicago: Albert Whitman, 1993.
> In this story, a father and son quiz each other on the traditions of 21 different African cultures.

Lacapa, Michael. *Antelope Woman*. Flagstaff, AZ: Northland Publishing Co., 1992.
> This is an illustrated Apache folktale of a beautiful woman who follows a mysterious young man who has come to teach her people respect for all things in nature. She eventually becomes his wife.

Lawton, Sandy. *Daddy's Chair*. Rockville, MD: Kar-Ben Copies, Inc., 1991.
> While sitting shiva during the Jewish week of mourning, Michael realizes that the family can share memories of his father by sitting in his chair.

Lee, Jeanne M. *Ba-Nam*. New York: Henry Holt & Co., 1987.
> In Vietnam there is a special day, called Thahn-Minh Day, for honoring ancestors. Nan is old enough to visit the graveyard for the first time. She learns her culture's rituals and that she needn't be afraid of the gravekeeper, an old, wrinkled woman with black-dyed teeth.

Lexau, Joan M. *The Rooftop Mystery*. Illus. by Syd Hoff. New York: Harper & Row, 1968.
> This mystery story for beginning readers involves a Black family's move to a new house just a few blocks from their old home.

Lionni, Leo. *Swimmy*. (2nd ed.). New York: Knopf, 1987.
> Some small fish are bullied by a big fish until they are cleverly organized to outwit him.

Lyon, George Ella. *Mama Is a Miner*. Illus. by Peter Catalanotto. New York: Orchard Books, 1994.
> A mother describes her job working as a miner.

Mack, B. *Jessie's Dream Skirt*. Carrboro, NC: Lollipop Power, 1979.
> Jessie is teased by his classmates when he puts on a skirt. His preschool teacher, an African American man, comes to his aid.

Martin, B., Jr. *I Am Freedom's Child*. Oklahoma City, OK: Bowmar, 1970.
> This is a story in rhyme about cultural diversity.

Maurey, Inez. *My Mother and I Are Growing Strong*. Berkeley, CA: New Seed Press, 1976.
> A Latina mother and daughter are left alone when the father is sent to jail. Together, they learn to live without him.

Maury, Inez. *My Mother the Mail Carrier/Mi Mama la Cartera*. Illus. by Lady McCrady. New York: Feminist Press, 1976.
> In this bilingual book, a 5-year-old describes the close relationship she has with her mother, a mail carrier, and tells about her mother's job.

McGovern, Ann. *Black Is Beautiful*. Photographs by Hope Wurmfield. New York: Four Winds, 1969.
> This is a book of simple words and photographs, illustrating the positive connotations of the word *black*.

Merriman, E. *Boys and Girls, Girls and Boys*. New York: Holt, Rinehart & Winston, 1972.
This story shows us there are many alternatives in gender conduct.

Morris, Ann. *Bread, Bread, Bread*. New York: Lothrop, Lee & Shepard Books, 1989.
This book offers a photographic tour of bread. It is a rich glimpse at the diversity of world cultures.

Morris, Ann. *Hats, Hats, Hats*. New York: Lothrop, Lee & Shepard Books, 1993.
A photographic tour of hats around the world.

Morris, Ann. *Loving*. Photos by Ken Heyman. New York: Lothrop, Lee & Shepard Books, 1990.
This book provides examples of the different ways love can be expressed, with emphasis on the relationship between parent and child.

Morris, Ann. *On the Go*. Photographs by Ken Heyman. New York: Lothrop, Lee & Shepard Books, 1990.
Photographs and simple text introduce devices used by people all over the world to make our lives easier.

Morris, Ann. *Tools*. Photographs by Ken Heyman. New York: Lothrop, Lee & Shepard Books, 1992.
This book discusses the ways in which people move from place to place, including walking, riding on animals, and traveling on wheels and water.

Moss, Thylias. *I Want to Be*. Illus. by Jerry Pinkney. New York: Dial Books for Young Readers, 1993.
Exciting words and images stretch the imaginations of children about what they want to be.

Mower, Nancy A. *I Visit My Tutu and Grandma*. Kailua, HI: Press Pacifica, 1984.
A biracial child learns many things from her two grandmothers, one Hawaiian, the other White.

Munsch, Robert, & Kusugak, Michael. *A Promise Is a Promise*. Toronto: Annick Press, 1991.
On the first warm day of spring, Allashua and her mother are more than a match for the wily Qallupilluit.

Newman, Leslea. *Saturday Is Pattyday*. Illus. by Annette Hegel. Norwich, VT: New Victoria Publishers, 1993.
Lesbian mothers separate and Frankie fears the loss of one of her parents. The story is written from the perspective that Frankie could be a son or a daughter.

Ormerod, Jan. *Sunshine*. New York: Morrow, 1990.
This is a lovely picture story of a little girl's morning: awakening, waking her parents, all the rituals which go into a family's preparing for the day.

Ortiz, Simon. *The People Shall Continue*. Illus. by Sharol Graves. San Francisco, CA: Children's Book Press, 1988.
An overview, past, present and future, of Native American history, written for young children.

Osofsky, Audrey. *Dreamcatcher*. Illus. by Ed Young. New York: Orchard Books, 1992.
An Ojibway baby sleeps and wakes among his intergenerational family.

Paterson, Katherine. *The Tale of the Mandarin Ducks*. Illus. by Leo and Diane Dillon. New York: Dutton, 1990.

A pair of mandarin ducks, separated by a cruel lord who wishes to possess the drake for his colorful beauty, reward a compassionate couple who risk their lives to reunite the ducks.

Pearson, P. *Everybody Knows That*. New York: Dial Books, 1984.
This book deals with and challenges the stereotyping of gender roles by children.

Pellegrini, Nina. *Families Are Different*. New York: Holiday House, 1991.
Adopted Nico, a young Korean girl, is unhappy that she doesn't resemble her parents. However, when she looks around her classroom, she realizes that families can come in many shapes, sizes, and colors.

Pinkney, Andrea. *Seven Candles for Kwanzaa*. Illus. by Brian Pinkney. New York: Dial Books, 1993.
The seven principles of Kwanzaa, as well as its Swahili words, are explained.

Pinkney, Gloria Jean. *Back Home*. Illus. by Jerry Pinkney. New York: Dial Books for Young Readers, 1990.
Eight-year-old Ernestine lives in a big city, but she is going back to the farm where she was born and where her mother grew up.

Polacco, Patricia. *Babushka's Doll*. New York: Simon & Schuster, 1990.
Babushka matches her granddaughter up with a doll that is naughtier than she is.

Polacco, Patricia. *Chicken Sunday*. New York: Philomel Books, 1992.
To thank Miss Eula for her Sunday chicken dinners, three children sell decorated eggs to buy her a beautiful Easter hat.

Polacco, Patricia. *Just Plain Fancy*. New York: Bantam Books, 1990.
This story is set in Lancaster County, Pennsylvania, and is about an Amish girl learning to understand and come to terms with her culture.

Polacco, Patricia. *The Keeping Quilt*. New York: Simon & Schuster, 1988.
This is the story of a quilt which has been passed from generation to generation. Russian and Jewish family traditions are depicted.

Polacco, Patricia. *Mrs. Katz and Tush*. New York: Bantam Books, 1992.
Mrs. Katz, a lonely Jewish widow, and Larnel, a young African American boy, realize the similarities of their cultural heritages.

Powers, Mary Ellen. *Our Teacher's in a Wheelchair*. Chicago: Albert Whitman, 1986.
This book describes the activities of Brian Hanson, who is able to lead an active existence as a nursery-school teacher despite partial paralysis that requires him to use a wheelchair.

Quinlan, Patricia. *My Dad Takes Care of Me*. Illus. by Vlasta van Kampen. Toronto: Annick Press, 1987.
Luke is ashamed that his father is unemployed and at home all the time, but learns that other children have fathers who stay at home and take care of them, too.

Quinsey, Mary Beth. *Why Does That Man Have Such a Big Nose?* Seattle: Parenting Press, 1986.
This book can help answer some of the many difficult questions that children ask about disabilities.

Rade, Bernice. *Where's Chimpy?* Chicago: Albert Whitman, 1988.
A little girl with Down's Syndrome goes through her day searching for a lost toy.

Raschka, Chris. *Yo! Yes?* New York: Scholastic, Inc., 1993.
> A White boy is alone and realizes that an African American boy wants to be his friend.

Ringgold, Faith. *Tar Beach.* New York: Crown, 1991.
> An African American girl dreams for her working-class family.

Roe, Eileen. *Con Mi Hermano/With My Brother.* Illus. by Robert Casilla. Scarsdale, NY: Bradbury Press, 1991.
> A preschool child tells of the many adventures he has with his older brother. The text is bilingual.

Rosenberg, Maxine R. *My Friend Leslie: The Story of a Handicapped Child.* New York: Lothrop, Lee & Shepard Books, 1983.
> This is the story of a friendship between two children, one with multiple handicaps.

Say, Allen. *El Chino.* Illus. by the author. Boston, MA: Houghton Mifflin, 1990.
> The true story of "Billy" Wong, a son of Chinese immigrants, who became an outstanding bullfighter. Black-and-white drawings depict the past, watercolors the present.

Say, Allen. *Tree of Cranes.* Boston, MA: Houghton Mifflin, 1991.
> The author recalls his childhood in Japan and his first celebration of Christmas.

Schlank, Carol Hilgartner, & Metzger, Barbara. *Martin Luther King, Jr.: A Biography for Young Children.* Churchville, NY: Rochester Association for the Education of Young Children, 1989.
> This book presents Dr. King's childhood in a way young children can understand.

Schotter, Roni. *A Fruit and Vegetable Man.* Illus. by Jeanette Winter. Boston, MA: Little, Brown & Co., 1993.
> Ruby Rubenstein has been the finest grocer on Delano Street for 50 years. Everyone in his multicultural neighborhood depends on him, especially the newly arrived immigrant Sun Ho, who helps Ruby and becomes his protege.

Scott, Ann H. *On Mother's Lap.* Illus. by Glo Coalson. New York: McGraw-Hill, 1972.
> In this Inuit family, a young boy is concerned that his mother's lap might not be big enough for both his infant sister and himself.

Scott, Ann H. *Sam.* Illus. by Symeon Shimin. New York: McGraw-Hill, 1967.
> This is the story of a young African American boy, Sam, and his very busy family.

Segal, Lore. *Tell Me a Mitzi.* Illus. by Harriet Pincus. New York: Farrar, Straus and Giroux, 1991.
> Three delightful stories about Mitzi and her little brother Jacob who live with their family in a large city.

Sendak, Maurice. *We Are All in the Dumps with Jack and Guy.* New York: Harper Collins, 1993.
> This story about homeless children and how they survive is particularly good for children who live in cities and see homeless people on the street.

Seuss, Dr. *The Sneeches.* New York: Random House, 1961.
> Some sneeches have stars on their bellies and think they're superior to their star-less cousins until a stranger turns the sneech community topsy-turvy and makes everyone truly equal.

Severance, J. *Lots of Mommies.* Carrboro, NC: Lollipop Power, 1983.
    Stereotypes collapse as three women with nontraditional jobs live together
    and raise a child.
Showers, Paul. *Your Skin and Mine.* Illus. by Kathleen Kuchera. New York: Harper
Trophy, 1991.
    The scientific basis of skin color are explained in a way that is easy to under-
    stand.
Simon, Norma. *All Kinds of Families.* Photographs by Joe Lasker. Chicago: Albert
Whitman, 1976.
    This book deals with a wide spectrum of families: nuclear, adoptive, divorced.
    It has multicultural illustrations.
Simon, Norma. *Why Am I Different?* Photographs by Dora Leder. Chicago: Albert
Whitman, 1976.
    This book stresses a positive attitude towards diversity as it deals with the
    many fears children have about being different.
Spohn, David. *Winter Wood.* New York: Lothrop, Lee & Shepard, 1991.
    In this book, a multiracial father and son chop wood for their stove in winter-
    time.
Steltzer, Ulli. *Building an Igloo.* Buffalo, NY: Firefly Books 1991.
    In this how-to photobook, an Inuit father and son build an igloo for shelter.
Steptoe, John. *Mufaro's Beautiful Daughters: An African Tale.* New York: Morrow, 1993.
    This story is based on a legend from Zimbabwe.
Steptoe, John. *Stevie.* New York: Harper & Row, 1969.
    A young boy resents his family's boarder until the boarder leaves.
Stock, Catherine. *Emma's Dragon Hunt.* New York: Lothrop, Lee & Shepard, 1984.
    Emma's grandfather, newly arrived from China, introduces her to the power
    of dragons.
Surat, Michele M. *Angel Child, Dragon Child.* Illus. by Vo-Dinh Mai. New York: Scholas-
tic Inc., 1989.
    This is the story of a Vietnamese child's transition to life in the United States
    and her longing for her mother who is still in Vietnam.
Takeshita, Fumiko. *The Park Bench.* Translated by Ruth Kanagy. Illus. by Mamoru
Suzuki. Brooklyn, NY: Kane/Miller Books, 1989.
    A Japanese-English story about a bench that provides pleasure for the many
    people who come by.
Tompert, Ann. *Grandfather Tang's Story.* New York: Crown, 1982.
    This is a story told with Chinese tangram puzzles about two foxes who change
    shapes.
Topping, Audrey. *The Rooster Who Understood Japanese.* Illus. by Charles Robinson.
New York: Scribner, 1976.
    A picture book about a Japanese American family and their bilingual
    menagerie, including a chicken named Mr. Lincoln.
Valentine, Johnny. *One Dad, Two Dads, Brown Dad, Blue Dads.* Illus. by Melody Sarecky.
Boston, MA: Alyson Publications, 1994.
    This book features Lou answering questions about his two blue dads and his
    friends discovering that blue dads are like other fathers.
Waber, Bernard. *Ira Says Goodbye.* Boston, MA: Houghton Mifflin, 1988.

Ira's best friend is moving away, and both boys are extremely sad.

Waber, Bernard. *Ira Sleeps Over.* Boston, MA: Houghton Mifflin, 1972.

Spending the night away from home, Ira wrestles with how to deal with his fear and finds out he's not alone.

Waber, Bernard. *You Look Ridiculous Said the Rhinoceros to the Hippopotamus.* Boston, MA: Houghton Mifflin, 1966.

A hippo who doesn't feel good about who he is tries on a variety of different animal parts to see if he likes himself better.

Walker, Alice. *To Hell With Dying.* Illus. by Catherine Deeter. New York: Harcourt Brace Jovanovich, 1988.

The author relates how old Mr. Sweet, though often on the verge of dying, could always be revived by the loving attention that she and her brother paid him.

Ward, Lelia. *I Am Eyes/Ni Macho.* Illus. by Nonny Hogrogian. New York: Greenwillow Books, 1978.

This is a bilingual book about the early morning as seen by a young child in Kenya.

Wheeler, Bernelda. *Where Did You Get Your Moccasins?* Winnipeg: Pemmican Publications, 1986.

In answer to his classmates' questions about his moccasins, a child describes how his grandmother made them.

Willhoite, Michael. *Daddy's Roommate.* Boston, MA: Alyson Publications, 1990.

After his parents' divorce, a young boy discovers that his father and the man his father now lives with are gay. He learns that being gay is another way to love someone.

Williams, Vera B. *Cherries and Cherry Pits.* New York: Greenwillow Books, 1986.

Bidemmi, an African American girl who lives in New York in an apartment building, uses pens and paints to illustrate the stories she tells. This set of stories is all about cherries.

Williams, Vera B. *More More More Said the Baby.* New York: Greenwillow Books, 1990.

Little Guy, Little Pumpkin and Little Bird are children of diverse heritage whose relatives love them more than anything. It is a colorfully illustrated story.

Williams, Vera B. *Something Special For Me.* New York: Greenwillow Books, 1983.

Rosa has difficulty choosing a special birthday present to buy with the coins her mother and grandmother have saved until she hears a man playing an accordion.

Winter, Jeanette. *Follow the Drinking Gourd.* New York: Knopf, 1988.

This is a picture book about one family's escape from slavery on the Underground Railroad.

Winter, Jonah. *Diego.* New York: Knopf, 1991.

This story about Mexican muralist Diego Rivera is told through miniature paintings.

Yarborough, Camille. *Cornrows.* Illus. by Carole Byard. New York: Putnam, 1992.

During "storytellin' time," when the children sit still and have their hair braided, the mother and great-grandmother tell the history of "cornrowing" hair in African culture.

Yashima, Taro. *Crow Boy.* New York: Viking Press, 1955.
> A young boy from the mountain area of Japan goes to a village to go to school and must gain the friendship of other students.

Zolotow, Charlotte. *William's Doll.* Illus. by William Pene du Bois. New York: Harper & Row, 1972.
> William's father gives him a basketball and a train, but these do not make him want a doll any less.

RESOURCES

Cooperative Children's Book Center. *Multicultural Literature for Children and Young Adults,* (3rd ed.). Madison, WI: University of Wisconsin–Madison & Wisconsin Department of Public Instruction, 1991.

Miller-Lachmann, Lyn. *Our Family, Our Friends, Our World: An Annotated Guide to Significant Multicultural Books for Children and Teenagers.* New Jersey: R. R. Bowker, 1992.

Rochman, Hazel. *Against Borders: Promoting Books for a Multicultural World.* Chicago: American Library Association, 1993.

Rollock, Barbara. *Black Authors and Illustrators of Children's Books: A Bibliographical Dictionary.* New York: Garland Publishing, 1992.

Many people helped with the compilation of this bibliography. My grateful thanks to Claudia Schwalm at Claudia's Caravan, Starr La Tronica at the Berkeley Public Library, Beverly Slapin at Oyate, Frederick Kasl, and Julie Silber.

References

Apple, M. (1992). The text and cultural politics. *Educational Researcher, 21* (7), 4–11.

Banks, J. A. (Ed.). (1973). *Teaching ethnic studies: Concepts and strategies* (Forty-third Yearbook of the National Council for the Social Studies). Washington, DC: National Council for the Social Studies.

Berger, J. (1992, December 3). A mix of earlier skirmishes converges in the rainbow curriculum battle. *New York Times, 142,* B4.

Bernstein, R. (1988, February 29). Twenty years after the Kerner Report: three societies, all separate. *New York Times, II, 8:1.*

Beuf, A. (1977). *Red children in white America.* Philadelphia: University of Pennsylvania Press.

Biber, B. (1977). A developmental–interaction approach: Bank Street College of Education. In M. C. Day & R. K. Parker (Eds.), *The preschool in action: Exploring early childhood programs* (2nd ed., pp. 423–460). Boston: Allyn & Bacon.

Biber, B., Shapiro, E., & Wickens, D. (1971). *Promoting cognitive growth.* Washington, DC: National Association for the Education of Young Children.

Bisson, J. (1992). Celebrating holidays in the anti-bias early childhood education program. Master's thesis, Pacific Oaks College, Pasadena, CA.

Bowman, B., & Stott, F. (1994). Understanding development in a cultural context. In B. L. Mallory & R. S. New (Eds.), *Diversity & developmentally appropriate practices* (pp. 119–133). New York: Teachers College Press.

Bredekamp, S. (1987). *Developmentally appropriate practice in early childhood programs serving children from birth through age 8.* Washington, DC: National Association for the Education of Young Children.

Brown, L. M., & Gilligan, C. (1992). *Meeting at the crossroads: Women's psychology and girls' development.* Cambridge, MA: Harvard University Press.

Bruner, J. (1976). Nature and uses of immaturity. In J. Bruner, A. Jolly, & K. Sylvia (Eds.), *Play: Its role in development and evolution.* New York: Basic Books.

Burgest, D. R. (1973). The racist use of the English language. *The Black Scholar, 5,* 37–45.

Burman, E. (1994). *Deconstructing developmental psychology.* London and New York: Routledge.

Chesler, M. A. (1967). *What happened after you desegregated the white school?* Atlanta: Southern Regional Council.

Chesler, M. A. (1971). Teacher training designs for improving instruction in interracial classrooms. *Journal of Applied Behavioral Science, 7,* 612–41.

Citron, A. (1971). *The 'rightness' of 'whiteness'—The world of the white child in a segregated society.* Detroit: Wayne State University, College of Education, Office of Urban
Education.

Cohen, D. H., Stern, V., & Ballaban, N. (1983). *Observing and recording the behavior of
young children* (3rd ed.). New York: Teachers College Press.

Cole, M. (1971). *The cultural context of learning and thinking.* New York: Basic Books.

Cole, M., & Cole, S. (1993). *The development of children* (2nd ed.). New York: Scientif-
ic American Books.

Cuffaro, H. K. (1995). *Experimenting with the world: John Dewey and the early childhood
classroom.* New York: Teachers College Press.

Delpit, L. D. (1986). Skills and other dilemmas of a progressive Black educator. *Harvard Educational Review, 56* (4), 379–385.

Delpit, L. D. (1988). The silenced dialogue: Power and pedagogy in educating other
people's children. *Harvard Educational Review, 58* (3), 280–298.

Derman-Sparks, L. (1989). *Anti-bias curriculum: Tools for empowering young children.*
Washington, DC: National Association for the Education of Young Children.

Derman-Sparks, L., Higa, C. T., & Sparks, B. (1980). Children, race, and racism: How
race awareness develops. *Interracial Books for Children Bulletin, 11* (3–4), 3–9.

Dugan, T. F., & Coles, R. (Eds.). (1989). *The child in our times: Studies in the development
of resiliency.* New York: Brunner/Mazel.

Gardner, H. (1991). *The unschooled mind.* New York: Basic Books.

Garmezy, N. (1991). Resiliency and vulnerability to adverse developmental outcomes
associated with poverty. *American Behavioral Scientist, 34* (4), 416–430.

Gay, G. (1973). Racism in America: Imperatives for teaching ethnic studies. In J. A.
Banks (Ed.), *Teaching ethnic studies: Concepts and strategies* (Forty-third Yearbook
of the National Council for the Social Studies, pp. 27–49). Washington, DC:
National Council for the Social Studies.

Gibson, P. (1989). *Report of the secretary's task force on youth suicide.* U.S. Department of
Health and Human Services.

Gilligan, C. (Ed.). (1990). *Making connections: The relational worlds of adolescent girls at
Emma Willard School.* Cambridge, MA: Harvard University Press.

Gold, M. J., Grant, C. A., & Rivlin, H. N. (Eds.). (1977). *In praise of diversity: A resource
book for multicultural education.* Washington, D.C.: Teacher Corps and Association
of Teacher Educators.

Goodman, M. E. (1952/1964). *Race awareness in young children.* (2nd ed.). New York:
Crowell-Collier. Original work published 1952.

Grossmann, K., Grossmann, K. E., Spangler, S., Suess, G., & Unzer, L. (1985). Mater-
nal sensitivity and newborn orientation responses as related to quality of attach-
ment in Northern Germany. *Monographs of the Society for Research in Child Development, 50* (1–2 Serial No. 209).

Hall, E. T. (1959). *The silent language.* New York: Doubleday.

Hall, E. T. (1966). *The hidden dimension.* New York: Doubleday.

Hirsch, E. (Ed.). (1974). *The block book.* Washington, DC: National Association for
the Education of Young Children.

Hirsch, E.D. (1987). *Cultural literacy: What every American needs to know.* Boston: Houghton Mifflin.

Hirsch, E. D. (1988). *Dictionary of cultural literacy.* Boston: Houghton Mifflin.

Holt, J. (1982). *How children fail.* New York: Dell.

hooks, b. (1984). *Feminist theory: From margin to center.* Boston: South End Press.

hooks, b. (1989). *Talking back.* Boston: South End Press.

hooks, b. (1990). *Yearning.* Boston: South End Press.

hooks, b. (1994). *Teaching to transgress.* New York: Routledge.

Hovey, F. (1975). *Ethnicity and early education.* Urbana, IL: ERIC Clearinghouse on Early Childhood Education (ERIC Document Reproduction Service No. ED 107 368).

Irwin, P. M., & Bushnell, M. M. (1980). *Observational strategies for child study.* New York: Holt, Rinehart & Winston.

John, V. P. (1972). Styles of learning—styles of teaching: Reflections on the education of Navajo children. In C. B. Cazden, V. P. John, & D. Hymes (Eds.), *Functions of language in the classroom.* New York: Teachers College Press.

Katz, J. H. (1978). *White awareness.* Norman: University of Oklahoma Press.

Katz, P. A. (Ed.). (1976). *Towards the elimination of racism.* New York: Pergamon Press.

Kochman, T. (1981). *Black and white styles in conflict.* Chicago: University of Chicago Press.

Kotlowitz, A. (1991). *There are no children here.* New York: Doubleday.

Kuroiwa, P. (1975). *The "invisible students."* Momentum, 6, *34–36.*

Lerner, G. (1988). *Black women in white America.* New York: Vintage Books.

Lieberson, S. (1980). *A piece of the pie: Blacks and White immigrants since 1880.* Berkeley: University of California Press.

Longstreet, W. S. (1978). *Learning and diversity: The ethnic factor.* Educational Research Quarterly, 2, 60–73.

Lubeck, S. (1994). The politics of developmentally appropriate practice. In B. L. Mallory & R. S. New (Eds.), *Diversity and developmentally appropriate practices* (pp. 17–43). New York: Teachers College Press.

McIntosh, P. (1995). White privilege and male privilege: A personal account of coming to see correspondences through work in women's studies. In M. L. Andersen & P. H. Collins (Eds.), *Race, class, and gender: An anthology* (pp. 76–87). Belmont, CA: Wadsworth.

Mercer, J. (1979). *SOMPA technical manual.* New York: Psychology Corporation.

Minuchin, P. P., & Shapiro, E. K. (1983). The school as context of social development. In P. H. Mussen (Ed.), *Handbook of child psychology: Vol. 4. Socialization, personality, and social development.* New York: Wiley.

Mitchell, L. S. (1971). *Young geographers.* New York: Bank Street College.

Morris, J. B. (1981). Indirect influences on children's racial attitudes. *Educational Leadership, 38,* 286–87.

New, R. S., & Mallory, B. J. (1994). Introduction: The ethic of inclusion. In B. L. Mallory & R. S. New (Eds.), *Diversity and developmentally appropriate practices* (pp. 1–13). New York: Teachers College Press.

Nicholson, S., & Shipstead, S. G. (1994). *Through the looking glass: Observations in the early childhood classroom.* New York: Macmillan.

Nicolopoulou, A. (1991). Play, cognitive development, and the social world: The research perspective. In B. Scales, M. Almy, A. Nicolopoulou, & S. Ervin-Tripp (Eds.), *Play and the social context of development in early care and education* (pp. 129–142). New York: Teachers College Press, 1991.

Nieto, S. (1992). *Affirming diversity: The sociopolitical context of multicultural education.* New York: Longman.

Opie, I., & Opie, P. (1969). *Children's games in street and playground.* London: Oxford University Press.

Orenstein, P. (1994). *School girls: Young women, self-esteem, & the confidence gap.* New York: Doubleday.

Pipher, M. (1994). *Reviving Ophelia: Saving the selves of adolescent girls.* New York: Ballantine Books.

Porter, J. (1969). *Black child, white child: The development of racial attitudes.* Cambridge, MA: Harvard University Press.

Powell, D. (1994). Parents, pluralism, and the NAEYC Statement on Developmentally Appropriate Practice. In B. L. Mallory & R. S. New (Eds.), *Diversity and developmentally appropriate practices* (pp. 166–182). New York: Teachers College Press.

Ramsey, P. G. (1979). Beyond "Ten Little Indians" and turkeys—Alternative approaches to Thanksgiving. *Young Children, 34,* 28–32, 49–52.

Ramsey, P. G. (1987). *Teaching and learning in a diverse world.* New York: Teachers College Press.

Random House unabridged dictionary (2nd ed.). (1993). New York: Random House.

Riessman, F. (1966). Styles of learning. *NEA Journal, 55,* 15–17.

Rollins, C. (Ed.). (1967). *We build together.* Champaign, IL: National Council of Teachers of English.

Roopnarine, J., Johnson, J., & Hooper, F. (1994). The need to look at play in diverse cultural settings. In J. Roopnarine, J. Johnson, & F. Hooper (Eds.), *Children's play in diverse cultures* (pp. 1–8). Albany: State University of New York Press.

Rosenthal, R. (1987). Pygmalion effects: Existence, magnitude, and social importance. *Educational Researcher, 16* (9), 37–41.

Rosenthal, R., & Jacobsen, L. (1968). *Pygmalion in the classroom: Teacher expectation and pupils' intellectual development.* New York: Holt, Rinehart & Winston.

Rutter, M. (1990). Psychological resilience and protective mechanisms. In J. Rolf, A. S. Masten, D. Ciccetti, K. H. Neuchterlein, & S. Weintraub (Eds.), *Risk and protective factors in the development of psychopathology* (pp. 181–214). Cambridge: Cambridge University Press.

Sadker, M., & Sadker, D. (1994). *Failing at Fairness: How our schools cheat girls.* New York: Simon & Schuster.

Saracho, O. N. (1993). Literacy development: The Whole Language approach. B. Spodek & O. N. Saracho (Eds.), *Language and literacy in early childhood education* (pp. 42–59). New York: Teachers College Press.

Shapiro, E., & Biber, B. (1972). The education of young children: A developmental—interaction approach. *Teachers College Record, 74,* 55–79.

Simonson, R., & Walker, S. (1988). Introduction. In R. Simonson & S. Walker (Eds.), *Multicultural literacy* (pp. ix–xv). St. Paul: Graywolf Press.

Sleeter, C. E., & Grant, C. A. (1994). *Making choices for multicultural education: Five approaches to race, class, and gender.* New York: Macmillan.

Smith, L. (1982). *The winner names the age: A collection of writings.* Michelle Cliff (Ed.). New York: W. W. Norton.

Spencer, M. B., & Markstrom-Adams, C. (1990). Identity processes among racial and ethnic minority children in America. *Child Development, 61,* 290–310.

Sprung, B. (1975). *Non-sexist education for young children.* New York: Citation Press.

Stabler, J. R., & Jordan, S. A. (1971). The measurement of children's self-concept as related to racial membership. *Child Development, 42,* 2094–97.

Statistical abstract of the United States 1994 (1994). Washington: U.S. Department of Commerce.

Stone, L. J., & Church, J. (1973). *Childhood and adolescence* (3rd ed.). New York: Random House.

Stritzel, K. (1995). Block play is for ALL children. *Child Care Information Exchange, 103,* 42–49.

Taba, H. (1955). *With perspectives on human relations.* Washington, DC: American Council on Education.

Taba, H. (1962). *Curriculum development: Theory and practice.* New York: Harcourt Brace Jovanovich.

Taba, H., Durkin, M. C., Fraenkel, J. K., & McNaughton, A. H. (1971). *A teacher's handbook to elementary social studies* (2nd ed.). Reading, MA: Addison-Wesley.

Terkel, S. (1992). *Race: How Blacks and Whites think and feel about the American obsession.* New York: New Press.

Trowbridge, G. (1995, Spring). Striking accord. In *Manhattan Country School's Public School Outreach & Gender Equity Projects, 2 ,* 1.

U.S. Commission on Civil Rights (1970). *Racism in America and how to combat it.* Washington, DC: Clearinghouse Publications, Urban Series No. 1.

Vygotsky, L. S. (1978). *Mind in Society: The development of higher physiological processes* (M. Cole, V. John-Steiner, S. Scribner, & E. Souberman, Eds. & Trans.). Cambridge, MA: Harvard University Press.

Walker, A. (1973). *Revolutionary petunias.* New York: Harcourt Brace Jovanovich.

Walker, A. (1984). *Horses make the landscape look more beautiful.* New York: Harcourt Brace Jovanovich.

Werner, E. E., Bierman, J. M., & French, F. E. (1971). *The children of Kauai.* Honolulu: University of Hawaii Press.

Williams, J. E., & Morland, J. K. (1976). *Race, color, and the young child.* Chapel Hill: University of North Carolina Press.

Wilson, G. (1980a). The word *nigger* is what's not allowed. *Interracial Books for Children Bulletin, 11* (3–4), 16–18.

Wilson, G. (Ed.). (1980b). Children, race and racism: How race awareness develops. *Interracial Books for Children Bulletin, 11* (3–4).

Wurzel, J. S. (1988). Multiculturalism and multicultural education. In *Toward multiculturalism: A reader in multiculturalism* (pp. 1–13). Yarmouth, ME: Intercultural Press.

Yonemura, M. V. (1986). *A teacher at work: Professional development and the early childhood educator.* New York: Teachers College Press.

Youngblood, C. E. (1979). Multicultural early childhood education. *Viewpoints in teaching and learning, 55,* 37–43.

Index

◆ About the Author

Frances E. Kendall is a consultant on organizational change, specializing in issues of diversity. She received her master's degree from Bank Street College of Education and her doctorate from the University of North Carolina at Chapel Hill. Her dissertation was on teachers' racial attitudes. Author of articles on multicultural education and communication issues in the workplace, she has consulted with all kinds of organizations including institutions of education ranging from child-care centers to colleges and universities.